Historic Preservation: Stories and Laws

HISTORIC PRESERVATION: STORIES AND LAWS

Shelby D. Green & Nicholas A. Robinson

Published by:

Vandeplas Publishing, LLC – April 2020

801 International Parkway, 5th Floor
Lake Mary, FL. 32746
USA

www.vandeplaspublishing.com

ISBN 978-1-60042-511-0

HISTORIC PRESERVATION: STORIES AND LAWS

SHELBY D. GREEN
&
NICHOLAS A. ROBINSON

Table of Contents

Preface

Care for history—whether found in personal memoires or in restoring great public places and monuments—is intrinsic to being human. Over the ages, societies world-wide have fashioned norms and procedures for managing their cultural and natural heritage. Across the United States, the nation's patrimony of historic buildings and sites is largely the responsibility of our cities, towns and villages. Local governments adopt and apply historic preservation law.

It is citizens who do this work. Historic preservation works well because civic leaders, history buffs, professional art historians and archaeologists, lawyers, architects, and a host of other professionals meet in the decision-making about how to sustain our historic built environment. We dedicate this book to them all.

We have been privileged to work with, and learn from, and teach many individuals who make historic preservation effective. Their endeavors have always been challenging, as the stories in this book illustrate. We thank them. In the coming years, however, they and all of us face an entirely new set of problems. The advent of harsh impacts on historic buildings and sites from the effects of climate change transforms the preservation models we have fashioned.

This book looks into the future about saving the past. It raises an initial agenda for topics that must be addressed to move the law of historic preservation into a new era, which many call the Anthropocene. Human ingenuity is manifest across cultural heritage, along with all the efforts to preserve the story of our past. The same resourcefulness will find the pathways into "Historic Preservation 2.0"—a new system that builds on what this book describes, but innovates beyond to marshal a regime that sustains the collective memories of our civilization. It is, after all, human to do so.

Shelby D. Green   Nicholas A. Robinson

Elisabeth Haub School of Law at Pace University
White Plains, New York

Chapter 1:
Philosophical Musings

1A. Caught in Time?

Humans have valued amber from time immemorial. Amber hails from prehistoric times, when ancient conifers thrived between 252 and 66 million years ago though the Pleistocene glaciation, the "Ice Age." Over time, resin from the conifers fossilized. In more recent centuries humans discovered and mined amber, valuing its translucence. Amber links humans to Earth's pre-human ages. In the aftermath of the Ice Age, artisans carved amber to create jewelry and other works of art, and architects incorporated amber in buildings.

Artifacts of amber are prominent in cultural heritage. An exquisite interior room encased in amber and gold was crafted in Germany and given by the King of Prussia to Tsar Peter the Great in 1716. This room was installed in a palace in Tsarskoye Selo, near St. Petersburg, which became the summer residence of the Tsars. Under the Soviet Union, the Catherine Palace and its amber room enjoyed legal protection as an historic landmark and museum. Nazi troops looted the palace in the Second World War and the room was lost. To recreate the amber room, the Soviet Union replicated this "wonder of the world" between 1979 and 2003 (at a cost of $11 million) and reinstalled it in the Catherine Palace. On the 300th anniversary of St. Petersburg, German Chancellor Gerhard Schroeder and Russian President Vladimir Putin commemorated the restoration and toasted a new era for their nations' international relations. The Amber Room today is safeguarded as a Russian State Museum and a World Heritage Site.

Amber also features significantly as part of natural heritage. It is a time capsule. Within its resins, amber captures and preserves ancient life forms. Amber archives of the Earth's natural past are still being discovered. In 2011, paleontologists in Canada found the first protofeathers of dinosaurs dating from the Cretaceous Period. Museums of Natural History preserve amber encased plants, insects and other life forms. Some places exhibit amber simply as a curiosity for tourism, such as the Amber Museum in Puerto Plata, Santa Domingo, which boasts the world's largest collection. Although amber opens past ages to contemporary human understanding, the sites where amber is mined, from Siberia to India and across Europe and North America, are afforded little to no legal protection. Paleontologists in India have called for legal protection of sites where amber and other fossils exist.[1] Mining is pursued to amass the prospective wealth. Little attention is paid either to the natural history of landscapes where amber is found or to the past and present human history of amber mining. These are stories yet to be told and places yet to be "preserved."

1B. HOLISTIC OUTLOOKS ABOUT CULTURE

How should society assess or conserve cultural and natural heritage—like Amber—that transcends the geological eras of life on Earth? Can today's policies and laws on historic preservation contribute to stewardship of such legacies?

In North America, the Laurentide Ice Sheet during the Pleistocene glaciation (2.58 million years ago) covered much of the continent. The ice produced the Great Lakes and shaped the eastern seaboard of the United States. Successive flows of glacial ice left massive moraines, and glacial till became places like Cape Cod, the easternmost point of the United States. As glaciers melted, their waters mingled with the oceans, flowing over the coastal plains and inundating once dry land, forming the shallows of the Georges Bank, an area rich in sea life. The glacially sculpted shorelines of Cape Cod became the home of the Wampanoag, the indigenous "people of the first light."

Wampanoag met the explorers from Europe, such as Samuel de Champlain, as they visited the Cape in 1605, and welcomed the Pilgrims who came to the Cape in 1620. Pilgrims left the Cape to settle at what became Plymouth Colony across Cape Cod Bay. Amber was rare here, although a deposit in 1883 was found in Nantucket Island off the Cape. Wampanoag valued wampum, the shell beads handmade from the purple and white portions of quahog clam shells, and from shells of the North Atlantic channeled whelk. Wampum provided the means

1 Sanjay Kumar, *India's Paleontologists Fight Destruction of its Fossil Riches*, Science, April 4, 2018, *https://www.sciencemag.org/news/2018/04/india-s-paleontologists-fight-destruction-its-fossil-riches.*

for memorializing important decisions. For example, it served as the symbols of leadership titles in indigenous communities, or for recording and sanctifying treaties, such as the celebrated Hiawatha Belt of Haudenosaunee (the seven nations of the people of the long house, whose union immigrants called the "Iroquois Confederacy"). Two Row Wampum Guswenta, a treaty between the Haudenosaunee and the Dutch, is still a living treaty guiding relations between the Onondaga and other Haudenosaunee nations and people who have come to their lands and waters since the 17th century. Wampum woven in belts can be read and conveys its message as does parchment, pen and ink in other cultural heritage contexts.

Human settlement on the shores of Cape Cod has changed over time. Those who came after the Pilgrims did not learn to read wampum. They harvested the pine and oak and cedar trees, and small communities stayed to farm and fish. Henry David Thoreau visited the Cape in 1849. He described the thinly-settled Cape as a place where the sea's waves and storms actively were shaping the coastal beaches. He visited the Highland Light, a lighthouse commissioned by George Washington in 1797. Impressed by Cape Cod's beauty, Thoreau predicted that future tourists and recreational facilities and summer residences would come to complement or supplant the fishermen and farmers and remnant Wampanoag:

> The time must come when this coast will be a place of resort for those New-Englanders who really wish to visit the sea-side. At present it is wholly unknown to the fashionable world, and probably it will never be agreeable to them. If it is merely a ten-pin alley, or a circular railway, or an ocean of mint-julep, that the visitor is in search of,—if he thinks more of the wine than the brine, as I suspect some do at Newport,—I trust that for a long time he will be disappointed here. But this shore will never be more attractive than it is now. Such beaches as are fashionable are here made and unmade in a day, I may almost say, by the sea shifting its sands. Lynn and Nantasket! this bare and bended arm is what makes the bay in which they lie so snugly. What are springs and waterfalls? Here is the spring of springs, the waterfall of waterfalls. A storm in the fall or winter is the time to visit it; a light-house or a fisherman's hut the true hotel. A man may stand there and put all America behind him.[2]

---

2 Henry David Thoreau, Cape Cod 252 (posthumous, 1865).

1C. EXPLORING TIME AND PLACE: CAPE COD

A century after Thoreau visited the Cape, much had changed. Geological forces continued to shape the Cape's Atlantic shores, eroding the bluffs along the beach by three feet each year. These processes threatened the very existence of the Highland Light, and in 1996 it had to be moved 450 feet inland. One can walk and bath on the Cape's still attractive and fashionable beaches, but they are not the same ones upon which Thoreau trod. The landscape of the Wampanoag and Pilgrim eras no longer existed by the time Thoreau arrived. Heathlands had emerged. Seventeenth- and eighteenth-century hamlets were replaced by Camp Edwards, a World War II defense and anti-aircraft training ground with seventeen barracks and later a Cold War radar installation. Most of these federal properties then disappeared, the munitions dumps cleaned up, to become part of the Cape Cod National Seashore's landscape. Visitors to this enormously altered landscape experience the continuing geological and ecological processes, but do not see the rich tapestry of its human past. The landscape remains beautiful in different ways, with different flora and fauna. Since Thoreau's visit, the sea shifting sands of time moved the location of Thoreau's beach 150 yards off shore.

Thoreau's prediction came to pass. Tourists and summer residents did come. Demographics also contribute a different kind of erosion. From the 1930s to the 1960s, Edward and Josephine Hopper spent summers in the adjacent Town of Truro and painted much of the landscape and buildings of Truro and Wellfleet. Many of Hopper's landscapes have become sites for new vacation homes. A substantial human migration onto the Cape was converting heathlands and forest into residential housing and associated commercial buildings. In response, President John F. Kennedy sponsored the creation of the Cape Cod National Seashore in 1961, and Congress established a protected area for 26,666 acres in the outer Cape. The National Seashore encompasses the site of a Wampanoag settlement at Nauset. Many of the Bauhaus "Modern Houses" are preserved within the National Seashore's bounds. The Seashore preserves sites painted by Hopper, but maturing pines and oaks transform and obscure the heath and sand dunes that Hopper captured in painting. Outside the Seashore, development in the Town of Truro is on-going. Some iconic Hopper sites have been adaptively reused, such as "Rich's House," which now houses the Truro Vineyard and a rum distillery. In 2018, Christie's, the auctioneers for David Rockefeller's estate, sold

Hopper's painting of "Rich's House" in Truro for $8.4 million. Rich's farm house, a water mill tower and a heritage tree, are voluntarily conserved. The town lacks a local landmarks ordinance.

The National Seashore encompasses much of the landscape around the adjacent Town of Wellfleet, where Thoreau spent a night in a fisherman's home on his walk of Cape Cod. While the Town of Truro's adjacent acres succumb to real estate development, there is less unprotected land to develop in and around Wellfleet. The National Seashore protects Great Island along Cape Cod Bay as well as remnant cedar swamps. The seashore's ponds and both fresh and salt water wetlands are essential to the Atlantic flyway of migratory birds. The National Seashore has averted building new homes along the coast, where the Atlantic Ocean continues to erode at least three feet of shore sands and move them northward, around the Cape's point into Cape Cod Bay, each year.

The geological force producing these sea shifting sands were at work when Wampanoag and Pilgrims were the only people on Cape Cod. Over time, these forces have accelerated, as sea levels began to rise in the 20th century. Waves and currents moved sands claimed from the Atlantic beaches around the tip of the Cape to fill in the harbors and shores of Bound Brook and Griffiths Islands in Wellfleet. Few homes remain there today where once thriving settlements were found in the 19th century. As access to the water ended, people dismantled their homes and floated them across to be relocated at the head of Wellfleet Bay. On the site of the former Bound Brook island's town schoolhouse, there is a small memorial on a glacial rock, "erected in grateful Remembrance of the Island School House 1924:"

Though few remain who once met here,
And scattered are afar and near,
With love they hold in memory still
The Island School House on the hill,
And gladly do they mark the spot
That it may never be forgot.

The Cape Cod National Seashore now protects this landscape overlooking Cape Cod Bay, where the likes of Lorenzo Dow Baker and Washington Irving Knowles grew up. Bound Brook island was chosen by Francis B. Biddle, United States

Attorney General during the Second World War and a judge on the Nuremberg Tribunal, as his summer residence, centered around one of the original homes in Bound Brook. The Biddle family and Trust for Public Land preserved the Biddle compound by transferring it to the National Seashore. It has been zoned for residential development. The National Park Service administers the National Seashore, which boasts more visits than other components of the National Park system.

But "protects" does not mean "preserves." Sea level rise will compete with the shifting sands to bring salt marshes and bay tide waters into the "sea level" spaces between the island that the glaciers had left. They will be changed. Even the wooden houses, many now listed on the National Register of Historic Places and marked with Wellfleet Town "Historic House" plaques, may not last. Wellfleet has not enacted an historic preservation ordinance, partially because the local culture seeks to keep the historic town streetscape "as is." The social sensibilities are to keep even the 20th century "modern" houses built by Bauhaus architects from Cambridge, such as Marcel Breuer, Serge Chermayeff or Paul Weindlinger, who summered in Wellfleet after World War II. These houses were inventoried in 2011. The Cape Cod Modern House Trust keeps up the houses situated within the Cape Cod National Seashore. But Cape Cod is in the path of Atlantic hurricanes, and periodically intense storms add to the annual erosion by radically reshaping the natural and the built environment along with coastlines. Both cultural and natural heritage are "unprotected."

1D. CARE FOR NATURAL AND CULTURAL HERITAGE

Ecosystems are resilient and their plant and animal components adapt to changed physical conditions and evolve. Buildings however need stewards, to keep them up and restore and replace their components as wear and tear and time claim their fabric, wood and paint and craftsmanship. Historic preservation benefits from the research of art and architectural historians, much reproduced by the National Park Service in the Secretary of the Interior's Standards for the Treatment of Historic Properties.[3]

3 Secretary of the Interior's Standards for the Treatment of Historic Properties, Technical Preservation Services, Department of the Interior, *https://www.nps.gov/tps/standards.htm.*

The emergence of today's historic preservation laws and practices in the second half of the 20th century is the product of a growing socio-political consensus that seeks to sustain memories and cultural heritage. Laws and practices for landscape conservation arrived in the late 19th century. Both social movements for historic preservation and nature conservation present a growing community commitment, ranging across all parts of the country, in favor of conscious policies and laws that sustain beauty and artistic achievement. Landmark buildings are designated and preserved. Protected landscapes are removed from economic development pressures. Historic districts protect patterns of architectural design from different time periods. The very name, "Historic Preservation," bespeaks the aim of the movement to safeguard the historic built environment and adjacent landscapes.

Despite the progressive success of preservationists, the opposition has also persisted. Preservationists, like conservationists, are still framed as being anti-development, and "bad" for the economy. Although such claims are not verifiable, they have long enjoyed a political popularity. Special interests, such as local real estate developers, object to efforts that retard maximizing the speculative value of new development. This is illustrated by the saga of the campaign to save the home of one of the nation's founding fathers, John Jay, in Rye New York, told in the next chapter.

These disputes cast as "either/or" are becoming a thing of the past. They are bound up in an ideological bias that extolls short-term development, and discounts any cultural or natural values that are not immediately monetized. Is time running out on this dichotomy? Will the memory of this contest become bound up in the detritus of climate change, like ancient life contained in the resins of amber?

Notwithstanding the push back from the administration of President Donald Trump to contemporary sensibilities, both nature conservation and stewardship of historic places appear comfortable and accepted, at least to their advocates and supporters. Both conservation and preservation resist the economic forces that seek to develop sites for new commercial buildings or for extracting oil and gas. There are, perhaps, those who would always seek short-term economic value from old and inefficient buildings or undeveloped landscapes. The aims of maximizing economic gain often conflicts with that of historic preservation or the more modest economic gains of adaptive reuse of an historic structure. Further, it is also important to note that there are those who deliberately destroy historic sites, in the course of warfare. The original Amber Room was likely lost in the bombing of Königsberg, Germany, in World War II.[4] Armed conflict at any level, time and place, destroys cultural heritage.[5]

Today we must acknowledge that *preservation versus development* controversies, although still raging, are becoming obsolete. So too, the competition that some see between historic preservation and environmentalism and nature conservation. All nature today is a part of cultural heritage and has a history. All landmarks exist in a landscape, even if there are many (not just the Trump Administration) that do not yet perceive this reality. The changes to the ambient environment accompanying climate change will make this apparent. The physical impacts associated with climate change make arguing about "preservation" or "development" and "conservation versus preservation" a "fool's errand."

Landmarks and the fabric of the built environment cannot be preserved in amber. A real estate developer's pretense to be able to build and sell a structure designed to last "forever" has become more of a "risk" than a certainty. New homes built along the shore at sea level in 2020, like long-built historic piers, fortifications or light houses, will not be immune to sea level rise. In the Anthropocene, the era of the 21st century, new approaches will be required to preserve the past. In 1983, the sandstone Temple of Dendur (Pharaonic era, 15 B.C.) was saved from the rising waters behind the Aswan High Dam and moved from the Nile Valley in Egypt to reside inside of the Metropolitan Museum of Art in New York City, preserved as if in amber. The permanence of any building may look like an insect frozen in the resin of amber. How many such preservations are today possible? Or tomorrow?

4 *See* Jess Bloomberg, *A Brief History of The Amber Room*, Smithsonian (July 21, 2007), *https://www.smithsonianmag.com/history/a-brief-history-of-the-amber-room-160940121/*.

5 *See* Robert Bevan, The Destruction Of Memory: Architecture at War (2006).

1E. WEATHERING THE GATHERING STORM

In the wake of "destruction" accompanying floods and sea level rise and other changes to the environment as we know it, will governments have the funding, artisans, and talent to restore the Amber Rooms that history so value? Can we develop an ethic that seeks to document and inventory today's historic monuments, so that we can preserve the memory of what we have lost as fully as possible? We have the digital capacity to do so, as never before. Can we leave space for evolutions of landscapes amidst changes produced by natural forces that we cannot control, as the Congress did when it set up the Cape Cod National Seashore? Can we facilitate the efforts of those who seek to move a landmark to a safer location, and recognize that *in situ* preservation is often an impossibility?

How can we decide what to move and when? When John D. Rockefeller, Jr. restored Williamsburg, Virginia, to its colonial era, he quietly acquired the properties and then began an 18th century restoration. He chose to eradicate post-colonial structures, including Civil War sites, thereby erasing 19th century stories found in that historic city. In 1893, the Town of Katonah was moved to make space for the Croton Reservoir, which flooded the town site. The buildings were moved to the "new" village of Katonah, and the historic fabric of the community was saved, much as the homes on Bound Brook Island in Wellfleet found new life in new locations. When Egypt built the Aswan High Dam, it saved many Pharaonic temples and donated a few to other countries, but many more were lost. These were "planned" historic preservation efforts. What of the unplanned, in the aftermath of storms or fires?

In 1996, after Chelsea City experienced fifteen floods in twenty-five years on the Iowa River, the City Council agreed to accept federal proposals that the entire town move to higher ground.[6] Residents at once objected to the loss of 130 years of history. When Chelsea's Sesquicentennial was observed in 2014, the City was "as is."[7] In the massive floods of 2019, the 300 residents continued to express

6 Keith Schneider, *15 Floods in 25 Years, Town's Moving*, New York Times (June 2, 1994), *https://www.nytimes.com/1994/06/02/us/15-floods-in-25-years-town-s-moving.html*; see also Susan Saulny, *A Town That Looked at Leaving the Flood Plain but Stayed On*, New York Times (June 17, 2008), *https://www.nytimes.com/2008/06/17/us/17iowa.html.*

7 Joyce Wiese, Chelsea Sesquicentennial—town history—a wealth of memories, Tama News-Herald (July 22, 2014), *http://www.tamatoledonews.com/page/content.detail/id/547888/Chelsea-Sesquicentennial--town-history---a-wealth-of-memories.html.*

loyalty to their town and opted to remain despite the floods.[8] It is not likely to be easy to shape a consensus about moving entire communities, with their historic buildings. The default setting is to "shelter in place." How long is such an approach sustainable? How many local landmarks will succumb to the impacts of extreme weather events?

Isle de Jean Charles in Louisiana presents a similar story. Ancestral home of the Biloxi-Chitimacha-Choctaw Tribe since 1955, this once extensive coastal island has lost 98% of its "dry" land. Remaining residents live on a strip of 320 acres. Chief Deme Naquin asserts that his people do not wish to abandon their ancestors and cultural heritage. The State of Louisiana secured a federal grant to move the community. The Tribe wishes to move its cultural practices, since they define the community as much as does the ties to the land. However, State and regional planners see obligations to move only people and buy a new place for them to live. They cannot "see" or value the intangible cultural heritage. Moreover, residents in the lands where resettlement would be situated came to oppose the plan.[9] While governments debate the fate of this indigenous people[10] and their disappearing homeland,[11] few efforts exist to preserve it through oral histories or other methods.[12]

The fates of Isle de Jean Charles, still in Louisiana or Chelsea, precariously in Iowa, shed new light on the problems that historic preservation have faced in St. Petersburg with its Amber Room, or Wellfleet, with its 18th century homes relocated from Bound Brook Island. How can we come to understand together what they have in common? What is the ethic that values and sustains historic places and traditions albeit amidst changing times? How can intangible cultural

8 *Iowa Town Floods Yet Again, https://www.kcci.com/article/iowa-town-flooded-yet-again/6337955.*

9 Julie Dermansky, *Critics Say State "Hijacked" Isle de Jean Charles Tribe's Resettlement Plan*, Truthout (April 24, 2019), *https://truthout.org/articles/critics-say-state-highjacked-isle-de-jean-charles-tribes-resettlement-plan.*

10 Ted Jackson, *On the Louisiana Coast, A Native Community Sinks Slowly into the Sea*, Yale Environment360 (March 15, 2018), *https://e360.yale.edu/features/on-louisiana-coast-a-native-community-sinks-slowly-into-the-sea-isle-de-jean-charles.*

11 Julie Dermansky, *Louisiana and Isle de Jean Charles Tribe Seek to Resolve Differing Visions for Resettling 'Climate Refugees'*, Desmog (Feb. 5, 2019), *https://www.desmogblog.com/2019/02/05/louisiana-isle-de-jean-charles-tribe-plans-resettlement-climate-refugees.*

12 Emmanuel Vaughan-Lee, *Isle de Jean Charles, https://www.globalonenessproject.org/library/films/isle-de-jean-charles.*

heritage be "preserved," whether within its physical context or beyond it if the historic structure or place is gone? What measures are most effective at keeping historic artistry accessible, in use, in our consciousness and culture?

Government can help, and ultimately perhaps is essential. But the ethic of valuing and sustaining the historical foundations of civilization must be taught to government and instilled in it by each generation. The learning, along with needed financing and other resources, comes slowly. Governments can learn, as is evidenced by the evolution of policies and programs for historic preservation of the National Park Service. Governments change and can forget as well.[13] When a physical building is protected, generations over time come to see and value and sustain the structure as part of their heritage. This legitimizes the nurturing roles by which governments provide a sustaining framework.

In Russia, despite revolutions and wars and vastly different political systems at different times, government has wondrously protected the Catherine Palace, kept now as a museum and World Heritage Site. In the Town of Wellfleet, Massachusetts, the federal government's conservation of the Cape Cod National Seashore has provided an amber-like setting within which stewardship of adjacent historic sites can be spared the avarice of new real estate development. There are other examples of governments as good stewards. The built environment of the Hamlet of Katonah, N.Y. was moved, not destroyed, because the City of New York paid for the move, thus government supported the transformation. In every instance, some historical heritage is lost or transformed. How can it be remembered too? During the Great Depression, in 1935 the Works Progress Administration (WPA)[14] launched the Historic Sites Survey and the Historic American Buildings Survey (HABS),[15] which inventoried and recorded the knowledge of America's historic structures. The WPA records became invaluable, for after the Depression and World War II, many of the structures were lost. The WPA Federal Music Survey recorded and preserved the intangible cultural

---

13 Garuy E. Machlis and Jonathan B. Jarvis, The Future of Conservation in America—A Chart For Rough Water (2018).

14 Emergency Relief Appropriation Act of 1935, 49 Stat. 115, 15 U.S.C. §728. The WPA was formed by executive order 7034, by President Franklin D. Roosevelt. The archives and publications by the Works Progress Administration (1938-1943) are found in the National Archives, *https://www.archives.gov/research/guide-fed-records/groups/069.html.*

15 Discussed below.

heritage of folk musicians, now long gone. In an age of climate change disruption, it will be important to bring digital technology to the sorts of tasks that the WPA undertook.

1F. THE FURTHER AGENDA FOR PRESERVATION?

Those who care about cultural heritage, at any scale from landscapes to small structures, together with intangible cultural heritage, will need to define for governments the support systems essential to adapt to the change. Otherwise, the incremental erosion of our historic fabric will be the handmaiden of the decline and loss of historic places and people. Society has many competing needs, especially in the wake of extreme storm surges along marine coasts or vaster inland inundations of wide flood plains. Unless provision is made now to anticipate the threats to historic sites that climate change puts in harm's way, these sites will be lost. Even if we rise to the occasion and are able to relocate and restore structures in safer places, and also move to encase our memories in today's digital amber of a "virtual reality," we shall have lost something. We, and our descendants, shall not touch, see, smell and experience much of our great cultural accomplishments. Passing on our memories and monuments to future generations is humbling, but perhaps it is the ethic that defines civilization.

1G. WHAT THIS BOOK IS ABOUT

This book explores the ways governments are learning to keep memories and monuments across the United States. Endangered landmarks are often saved at the last minute. The Jay Property in New York is a prime example of this phenomenon. In the Anthropocene, to catch an historic site in the nick of time before its destruction, will require innovation. Those who value cultural and natural heritage alike will need to envision anew the tools, policies and laws that sustain cultural heritage. This book would stimulate a modest dialogue toward that end. How shall those of us who value sustaining historic memory do so through safeguarding landmarks and historic structures and landscapes? What steps are needed to move the contemporary consensus behind historic preservation to an uncertain time when all landmarks situated in the intertidal coastline are at risk? We do not know, but we invite you to share with us the many questions that we all face.

As a society, we are barely inside the threshold of tomorrow. The analogue of memory is foresight. We can look ahead remembering what we know today and learned from sustaining our knowledge of yesterday. The stories of historic preservation law are a prelude to the future.

Chapter 2:
John Jay: Whose Legacy?

2A. JOHN JAY, THE FOUNDER

In 1979, a small band of preservationists (The Jay Coalition) caught the Peter Augustus Jay Mansion (1838) just in time. It had become a ruin, an eyesore, to be forgotten. Some said, "better demolish it." In 2020, more than four decades later, it is celebrated as an American treasure. The preservation of this iconic family property of John Jay is a study in the never-ending effort to cherish, interpret and conserve our past, enabling future generations to do the same. While this story illustrates the short-comings of preservation law, it offers optimistic insights about keeping the monuments of our past.

This landmark in Rye, New York, and the surrounding landscape, is where founding father John Jay was raised and is buried, and where generations of his descendants lived. A real estate developer bought and allowed the historic Greek revival Mansion and other buildings on the site to deteriorate in hopes of demolishing them. The site was left open and unprotected. The Mansion lost its front door and other interior fixtures to pilferers. As a ruin, it was rented out to a filmmaker, who trashed the interior to shoot a horror movie. The grounds were overgrown and obstructed the view of the site from the adjacent Boston Post Road. The developer applied to demolish the buildings and construct a residential condominium project on the twenty-four acres. Preservationists stopped the demolition, but it would take until 1995 before the site was "saved."[1] It would take additional decades to begin a restoration. In 2020, the Jay Heritage Center, led by Suzanne Clary, is continuing its now historic mission to restore and sustain the Jay Property as an invaluable part of America's national cultural heritage.[2]

---

1 The saga of the legal issues involved in the campaign to save the Jay Property is told in Nicholas A. Robinson and Shelby D. Green, Historic Preservation—Law And Culture (2018).

2 *See* the Jay Heritage Center's website at *https://jayheritagecenter.org*.

John Jay is celebrated for his lifetime of public service. The diversity and breadth of his accomplishments are extraordinary and unique: as an author of the Federalists Papers; as president of the Second Continental Congress; as America's Secretary of Foreign Affairs (the post becoming the Secretary of State); as America's Minister to Spain and the diplomat who negotiated the Treaty of Paris (Jay Treaty) settling the revolutionary war between the new United States and the British Kingdom, and inventing the use of international "arbitration" to settle disputes; as a draftsman of the New York State Constitution, which served to guide Madison in his drafting of the later United States Constitution; as founder in 1787 of the Manumission Society to end slavery; as Governor of the State of New York; and as a judge in New York and the first Chief Justice of the United States Supreme Court. He literally created the legislative, executive and judicial branches in which he served and shaped America's first foreign policy.[3]

Some opine that John Jay is today the "neglected" founding father because the public does not have a nationally recognized home, like Monticello, Mt. Vernon or Montpelier, to visit. Whatever the reason, the nation owes John Jay greater continuing appreciation. John Jay's contributions to America merit a grateful remembrance. In 1989, during the Bicentennial of the United States Constitution, Chief Justice Warren E. Burger, joined a group of local preservationists and politicians, pronouncing that "To preserve the Jay Property would be an appropriate memorial to this important Founding Father during the bicentennial of the Constitution."[4]

The Jay Coalition labored on many fronts to restore the memory of John Jay's youth in Rye, to enable historians, Jay biographers, and everyone to visit and learn first-hand the place of Jay's formative youthful years. As memory of the Jay years in Rye is collected, it will contribute to our understanding of this founding father's uniquely conservative courage, his sense of justice, and his acutely honed conception of the rule of law. These attributes of the mature John Jay were essential to securing the independence of New York and other colonies from Britain, and to establishing the new federal government. Visiting his youthful haunts, experiencing what he did, opens new depths of understanding.

3 Richard B. Morris, John Jay, The Nation and The Court (1967); John Jay Papers, Richard B. Morris (ed) (Columbia University).

4 Tom Anderson, *U.S. Commission Backs Jay Property Preservation*, The Daily Item (Rye, NY), p. 1, (January 27, 1989).

2B. NO NEED TO SAVE THE JAY PROPERTY?

John Jay's father, Peter Jay was a Huguenot and his mother, Mary van Cortland was Dutch. They moved their family into the country, bringing John Jay, then a three month-old infant, to Rye to escape the small pox epidemics in Manhattan.[5] Peter Jay bought 250 acres along Long Island Sound. Ships were the reliable transportation of the day. The family called his two-story farm house, "The Locusts." John Jay grew up in Rye, before attending Kings College (now Columbia University) in New York City. His brother Peter Augustus Jay built a larger home for the family on the site of the first farmhouse. The Locusts held the Jay family's burial ground, a private family cemetery where John Jay with his ancestors and descendants rest today. John Jay later reconstructed the "Locusts" of his youth in the nearby Town of Bedford, New York, where he retired after his historic career.

The landscape of John Jay's home is unique. Here are found the relics of the Siwanoys, indigenous people who dwelt along the shores of Long Island and fished and hunted on these lands as long as 3,000 years ago. There is also the architectural heritage of Jay's family as well as of later affluent owners of the estate. One of Jay's descendants, Mary Rutherford Jay, was the landscape architect for gardens at the property. The site offers an undisturbed window into the lives of enslaved persons and illustrates the struggles to end slavery in New York. The rapid economic development after World War II saw much of the Jay Property turn into residential housing, but that in turn inspired donations of remaining natural acres for conservation. The landscape of the Jay Property is largely unchanged, leaving an archaeological heritage accessible, while its landmark buildings are beacons for recalling the lives of their inhabitants.

Founded in 1694, the City of Rye is proud of its history. The Rye Historical Society is housed in Squire House, a colonial tavern visited by John and Samuel Adams and George Washington. Curiously, even in 2020, the Society does not celebrate any of the Jay family members' inevitable visits.[6] In Rye's three and a half centuries of development, it has lost most of its countryside, and much

5 John Jay biograohy at Jay Hertiage Center, *https://jayheritagecenter.org/about/history-of-the-jay-estate/john-jay/.*

6 See Squire House Museum/Rye Historical Society, *https://paththroughhistory.iloveny.com/listings/Square-House-Museum-Rye-Historical-Society/32350/#.XSDMhC2ZOu4.*

of its colonial past has been absorbed into the fashions of the 18th, 19th, and 20th centuries of architectural heritage.

Rye first began identifying landmarks with honorary designations, but affording no legal protection. In 1977, Rye enacted its first landmark law. It provided that owners had to consent to any landmark designation and did not provide for regulation of landmarks as did the New York City Landmarks Preservation Law.[7] It was not until 1983, that the City of Rye amended its local code to require owners of landmarks to apply for a "Certificate Of Appropriateness" that would protect historic values.[8] Although the United States Supreme Court upheld the constitutionality of such regulations in 1978, as described in the next chapter, Rye's City Council was reluctant to amend its local laws to do so because of the raging controversies in the battle between a real estate developer and the preservationists over the fate of the Peter Jay Mansion and surrounding landscape. Rye was slow to defend the Jay Property because memory of the Jay family links to Rye had faded. Jay descendants sold the Jay Property in 1905, reserving the Jay cemetery. The Mansion was the center of an estate known as "Alansten," one of three adjacent great estates situated along the Boston Post Road, overlooking Long Island Sound across a meadow that the Siwanoys and their ancestors had burned to clear and keep open for hunting, in the centuries before the Jays came. Owners after the Jays added buildings, including one of America's first indoor tennis arenas. The Van Norden family built an elegant carriage house in 1912, and installed extensive gardens. After World War II, former Jay lands situated south of the Jay Property and west across the Boston Post Road, were sold to become single family homes. To the northeast and east, Parsons family members donated adjacent forested lands and meadows and a stream that once served the Jay Property to Westchester County to become a local nature park, known as "Marshlands Conservancy." Zilph Palmer donated 120 acres in 1967 and in 1978 Fanny Wickes Parsons gave an additional 17 acres. Preserving this natural landscape also kept open the vista from the porch of the Peter Jay Mansion, down to Long Island Sound and beyond.

In 1966 the Methodist Church bought the remnant 24-acre Jay Property as a place to hold religious retreats. By 1979, it had applied to subdivide the site, with

7 Discussed in Chapters 3 and 4.

8 City of Rye Code, Ch. 117, Landmarks Preservation, *https://ecode360.com/6973425.*

six acres for the religious center and 17 acres for development, but Rye disapproved the plan and the Church sold the entire property to FGL&L Properties. This developer discontinued use of the Peter Jay Mansion and other buildings, and prepared development plans that did not preserve the old buildings. The developer planted a hedge row of trees adjacent to a ha-ha, the landscape feature that keep sheep or other animals in the pasture area. The hedge row ran along the border with the Marshlands Conservancy, so the view of the Mansion was obscured from the parklands, as was the vista across Long Island Sound from the porch.

The battle for Jay's heritage would now be waged over the fate of the last ten percent of the lands and buildings that John Jay knew as he grew up in Rye. During much of Jay's lifetime of public service he had to live away from Rye. When he retired, Jay had wanted his relatives to continue to live on the lands that his parents had bought and cared for by his family. Rather than relocating his brother's family when he returned to live in Rye, John Jay decided to build a new home for his retirement years on land that his mother's family, the van Cortlands, held in Bedford, New York. After Jay died, this home was lived in for generations by Jay's descendants. It finally was acquired by Westchester County, which being unable adequately maintain it, transferred the site to the State of New York.[9] Known as the John Jay Homestead, it is now a state historic site.[10] The Friends of the John Jay Homestead, a non-profit society, provide essential support for education and care of the Homestead.

Preservation of the John Jay Homestead in Bedford ironically contributed to public amnesia about Jay's years in Rye. FGL&L Properties, led by Diane Millstein, repeatedly argued that the Jay Property was not historically important, and that the Jay heritage was adequately preserved in Bedford. New York State officials and the Friends of the John Jay Homestead knew little about the Peter Jay Property in Rye and had their hands full caring for the Homestead. Choosing to discount any historic significance of the Rye property, Diane Millstein applied to rezone the property to build 220,000 square feet of office space. The new use, surrounded by residential and park uses, was opposed by

9 State of New York, Office of Parks, Recreation & Historic Preservation, *https://parks.ny.gov/historic-sites/4/details.aspx.*

10 John Jay Homestead, *https://ecode360.com/6973425.*

Rye officials. Eventually, she proposed subdividing the site into a residential use, with condominium apartments in the Peter Jay Mansion, and a dense cluster of residences along both sides of the open vista abutting the Marshlands Conservancy. This plan appeared to "save" the exterior of the Peter Jay Mansion and, while it encroached greatly on the historic viewshed, it did preserve that amenity too. By 1992, as DMG Partners, Diane Millstein was poised to secure Rye's approval for developing the site. The Jay Coalition feared that she was about to win the battle to erase most traces of the Jay legacy.

2C. CRAFTING A TOOLKIT OF LAWS

The citizens who fought to save the Jay Property, were a coalition: Rhoda M. Kornrich and Kitty Aresty were preservationists, dedicated to saving the Greek Revival landmark and other historic buildings; Catherine Crean was a conservationist committed to preventing erosion of the Marshlands Conservancy; Helen "Dee Dee" Pascal and Sharon du Bois fought to uphold John Jay's legacy and for protecting the Jay cemetery. There were many more women in this team, and it kept growing, extending beyond the City of Rye and Westchester County. These leaders reached out and enlisted Russell Cecil, Joseph T. Aresty, Professor Nicholas Robinson, who taught preservation law at Pace University School of Law, the former Congressman for the District, Hon. Richard L. Ottinger, and David Parsons, whose family owned the landmark estate adjacent to the Jay Property, among others. The Jay Coalition became a familiar voice and a political force.

Lacking an effective municipal landmarks law in Rye until 1983, over time, the Jay Coalition cobbled together a kit of legal tools, not one of which alone could save the Jay Property. As these citizens invoked each of their "rights," they caught the attention of the local news media (this was before the Internet).[11] Through newspapers, public hearings, newsletters, and talks with other civic

11 *The New York Times* from time to time covered the battles, and reported on their successful outcome. *See*, e.g. Roberta Harrison, "After Years of Conflict, Jay Sites Are Opening to the Public (April 28, 1996), at *https://www.nytimes.com/1996/04/28/nyregion/after-years-of-conflict-jay-sites-are-opening-to-the-public.html?mtrref=www.google.com&gwh=E831888454C42952FAB75FA00B11E66B&gwt=pay*; and Joseph Berger, "What's A Historic House You Can't Enter In Style?" (March 2, 2008), at *https://www.nytimes.com/2008/03/02/nyregion/nyregionspecial2/02colwe.html?mtrref=www.google.com&gwh=AF2043665D50850FC276BF0A768CA193&gwt=pay.*

organizations, the Jay Coalition was able to "teach" the public about Jay and his years in Rye. They assembled more than seventy local historical societies, conservation organizations, and civic groups, whose boards each called for preservation of the Jay Property. They sought testimonials and endorsements from pubic figures. They exercised their First Amendment right to petition government for the redress of grievances and to speak out.

After collecting all available historic documentation about John Jay in Rye and the Peter Jay Mansion, as well as the van Norden Carriage house and other structures at the Jay Property, the Jay Coalition used a series of legal maneuvers that proved effective to halt the development of the site. The first was to get the area listed on the National Register of Historic Places. Because the Boston Post Road (US Route 1) in Rye has three adjacent historic estates, and boasts a postal mile marker that Postmaster General Benjamin Franklin had placed in the stone wall at the Peter Jay Mansion, the Jay Coalition prepared a request that the "Boston Post Road Historic District" be created and listed. This listing ensured that, under Section 4(f) of the federal Transportation Act, no federally funded highway project would be allowed if it would impair the historic values of the District.[12] On the local level, the Jay Coalition petitioned the City of Rye to complement this federal listing by establishing under the City's zoning authority, the "Alansten Historic District," with protections for the viewway from the Peter Jay Mansion across the Marshlands Conservancy and back. The 1983 amendment to the landmark law would require a Certificate of Appropriateness ("COA") for alternations to local landmark buildings and the City Council further directed that only residential ownership would be allowed in the Alansten Historic District.

Diane Millstein challenged these maneuvers in a series of lawsuits. Eventually, New York's highest court in 1985 ruled that the City could not require a type of ownership, but could require a COA.[13] In a parallel case, the City's right to eliminate "owner consent" and require the COA was upheld.[14] Having failed in

12 49 U.S.C. 303(c) provided that a highway project could be funded if it posed harm to an historic site only if there was no "feasible and prudent" alternative. The importance of this act and restrictions had recently been underscored by a United States Supreme Court ruling in *Citizens to Preserve Overton Park v Volpe*, 401 U.S. 402 (1971). The case is discussed below in Chapter 8.

13 *FGL&L Property Corp. v. City of Rye*, 485 N.E. 2d 986 (N.Y. 1985).

14 *DMG Partners v. City of Rye*, No. 4609/85 (Sup. Ct., West. Co., July 10, 1985).

attacks on the legitimacy of the new Rye landmarks law, the developer applied for a COA, and sought demolition of the Peter Jay Mansion. When this application was found not to be historically appropriate, and that the building retained economic value, she sued the City, only again to lose in the courts.[15] Rye and the developer were now locked in a set of lawsuits about the design and density of her proposed site plans to develop the 24 acres.[16] She finally claimed that the City's restrictions were a regulatory taking of her property requiring compensation, but lost this argument also.[17]

The efforts to restore the contours of Jay's childhood years continued. Could the Jay Coalition, with its meagre finances, volunteer lawyers, and abundant civic energy, realize its goal of 100% preservation? Would Diane Millstein realize her goal of 100% development?

2D. DOES OWNERSHIP BY THE GOVERNMENT SAVE HISTORY?

When the City of Rye finally determined that it had no alternative, it approved a site plan for DMG Partners, which clustered housing units around the Peter Jay Manson, and retained a narrowed vista to Long Island Sound. The subdivision allowed an appraisal establishing the fair market value of her development project, if it was ever to be built. At this point Diane Millstein signaled to the Jay Coalition that she would consider sale of the site. Was this a hollow offer, knowing that the Jay Coalition lacked funds to buy the site? Had she tired of her battles and the prospect of dealing with the City of Rye and the Jay Coalition over a still contested development? Had she come to recognize that John Jay's home and legacy deserved restoration? Although the Jay Coalition had not the cash to buy her out, and the City of Rye had not the political will do so, the Coalition knew that either New York State or the County of Westchester might muster the will and the cash.

15 *DMG Partners v. Board of Architectural Review*, 148 A.D. 2d 608, 539 N.Y.S. 2d 7 (App. Div. 2d Dep't 1989).

16 The Rye City Corporation Counsel. Richard M. Gadelle, recounts these suits in "The Jay Mansion Preservation Case History," 21 Westchester Bar Journal 109 (1994)

17 DMG Partners-Rye v. City of Rye, 575 N.Y.S. 2d 330 (App. Div. 2d Dep't 1991). v.

The Coalition appealed to New York Governor Mario M. Cuomo and the Westchester County's Board of Legislators. Governor Cuomo offered $4 million through state agencies, if the County would pay the balance, a sum of $11.5 million. Diane Millstein exempted from her proffered deal, the Peter Jay Mansion and the Van Norden carriage house, which she would give to the Jay Coalition. Neither the state nor the county relished spending millions to restore these two landmarks. The citizens had raised funds to fight the battle to save them, and now would commit to raising the funds necessary to preserve them. The leaders of the Jay Coalition formed a non-for-profit corporation, the Jay Heritage Center ("JHC"), to take title to these buildings, with easements for access. The women on both sides had developed a kind of begrudging respect for each other. Neither quite trusted the "government."

However, negotiations over the purchase of the 24 acres around the Pater Jay Mansion and carriage house were more problematic. The county, its legislators and Parks Department, and the New York State Office of Parks, Recreation and Historic Preservation, had different perceptions of their authority and budgets. Both were reluctant players in drama. Neither had planned to have to buy the Jay Property. When agreement could not be reached on a price, the county Board of Legislators agreed to take the site by eminent domain. At the same time, DMG Partners-Rye filed a federal law suit claiming $60 million in damages, for among other things, inverse condemnation; while not explicitly pleading a conspiracy, the developers claimed the City engaged in a scheme to render their property unmarketable through regulation and the threat of condemnation. Eventually, condemnation was avoided and the federal "regulatory takings" claims were abandoned. The sale was consummated. By some estimates, the developers invested $2 million for the property purchase and expenses in planning for alternative development schemes and were paid $12 million.

When the State of New York[18] and Westchester County[19] took possession of the 24 acres surrounding the Peter Jay Mansion, the site was "saved." The public had educated the governments about the need to do so. Having enjoyed no maintenance for nearly three decades and having been victims of vandalism (a clock

18 As of July 4, 2019, the site is listed by New York State Office of Parks, Recreation & Historic Preservation, *https://parks.ny.gov/historic-sites/39/details.aspx.*

19 As of July 4, 2019, the site is listed by Westchester County, *https://parks.ny.gov/historic-sites/39/details.aspx.*

had been stolen from the cupola above the carriage house, a front door taken), the landmark structures were caught at the last minute before what amounted to their demolition by neglect. This success, however, was prelude to another two decades of struggles by citizens to hold the State and County governments to their obligations to safeguard the Jay Property.

When New York State and Westchester County purchased the site, the State established conditions for its maintenance and agreed for Westchester County to have possession of the entire site, except of course for the Peter Jay Mansion and the Carriage House. In the purchase of the estate, the County undertook to cooperate with the JHC in planning for the uses of the 24 acres around the landmarks, but this was half-hearted. The Westchester County Parks Department ("County Parks") had no real interest in investing in the costly restorations of buildings and their leaders expressed doubt that anyone would invest in stabilizing and restoring the derelict structures. Under the dedicated leadership of Suzanne Clary, of the JHC, combining the roles of president and executive director, the JHC and its board and other volunteers developed the vision and capabilities to interpret, restore, and conserve the entire landscape and its landmarks. As the public learned of the JHC's efforts, cooperation and support emerged. The mahogany front door of the Peter Jay Mansion was returned. The clock was found in an antique shop, returned and installed back into the tower of the carriage house. Jay family members became actively involved in restoration, donating furnishings from the Peter Jay Mansion that had remained in the family. Suzanne Clary and her board had built momentum for a culture of stewardship for cultural and natural heritage.

From the beginning, the JHC volunteers launched a multi-pronged effort to assemble documentation about all aspects of the site, including its prehistoric aspects. They sought out experts in architecture, art history, historic restoration, archaeology, ecology, biography, local history, social history including the Jay family efforts to end slavery, diplomatic history, legal history and applications of environmental law and historic preservation law, along with a host of other fields of expertise. The JHC raised the funds for archaeological digs and listed the site on the African-American Heritage Trail. In restoring the exterior and interiors, the JHC adhered closely to the Secretary of the Interior's Standards for the Treatment of Historic Properties. Slowly, deliberately, and as fund-raising permitted, the JHC stabilized the landmarks and began the painstaking restoration of the facades. They raised several million dollars.

Not only did the County Parks Department not fulfill its undertaking to assist with the management of the Jay Property, it engaged in acts calculated to frustrate the restoration—installing buffers between the adjacent historic sites; letting brambles grow tall along the ha-ha, that obscured the views of the Peter Jay Mansion from the Marshlands Conservancy; attempting to merge the Jay Property with the Marshlands Conservancy, erasing the distinct attributes of the Jay Property; and deliberately dumping wastes and other pollutants on the land and in the historic pool. The County Parks' antics left the JHC landmark building like fossils, encased in amber. County Parks chose not to see the sites in the context of their historic landscape. Taking its stewardship responsibilities seriously, the JHC sued the county, ably represented, *pro bono publico,* by the law firm of Cravath, Swaine & Moore, through Richard W. Clary, Esq., and his colleagues. The suit alleged that between 2000-2002, the JHC had completed a cultural landscape report for the acres of the Jay Property and Marshlands Conservancy, but that the County Parks had allowed woodlands to encroach on the historic meadow and had failed to maintain its open flora. Admitting that it could not devote resources needed to care for the 21.4 acres of Jay Property, County Parks agreed to turn over control of these acres to the JHC. For the first time, the JHC could plan for a fully integrated stewardship of the cultural and natural landscape. Since then, the JHC has identified elements of Jay history including farming sites, the probable location of slave quarters and a burial ground and has restored the footprint of later formal gardens. Unfortunately for the JHC, County Parks continue to frustrate its thoughtful preservation and conservation of the site. Without consulting with the JHC or the Parson family, County Parks proposed a sort of development—to widen the road and pave it (from a small lane leading to the Jay Family Cemetery) to allow school buses to enter the Marshlands Conservancy, construct a large new parking lot adjacent to the Jay Property, to serve a newly built visitor's center to be used for both administrative offices and educational programs. The new building was to be adjacent to the meadow and directly in view of the Peter Jay Mansion porch. From this porch, for the past 300 years, one can enjoy the same view across fields and forests and seascape to distant Long Island. County Parks' building plans would break this historical landscape, not unlike Diane Millstein's condominium project would have. County Parks preferred to build up Marshlands

Conservancy to serve other of Parks' education missions. Parks had lost track of the Parson family members' wishes that the Marshlands Conservancy be kept as an undeveloped nature conservancy.

County Parks' plans were included in its budget requests to Westchester County and approved as routine upgrades for the Marshlands Conservancy. At the last minute, JHC learned about these plans. Not only had County Parks launched its project without notice to JHC or other neighbors, it had made no environmental impact assessment for this project. For the second time, the JHC was obliged to sue. Professor Shelby D. Green, a member of the JHC Board of Directors, and Professor Nicholas A. Robinson, met with Jay descendants, cemetery trustees, David Parsons, and JHC volunteers to scope out how County Parks was in violation of its legal obligations for both cultural and natural heritage. Once again, Cravath, Swaine & Moore represented JHC in presenting a new round of legal claims to Westchester County. The Westchester County Executive heard JHC's concerns and blocked the plans.

Now, the 24 acres of the Jay Property, with the 150 natural acres of the Marshlands Conservancy, can be sustained and interpreted in all the diversity of their intertwined natural and cultural history. That knowledge and memory can also be erased. County Parks elected to erase the holistic vision when selecting its preferred concept about how the public should be experiencing nature. One tragedy of erasing history is that it diminishes us all. We never know what we have lost. This sort of ahistorical approach offended the JHC's leadership. JHC proffers a richer, and more complex and nuanced understanding of this landscape in Rye:[20]

> As a member of England's Royal Horticultural Society, John Jay eagerly shared his passion for planting trees with his American colleagues and his children, regularly sending them seeds from his travels in Europe. Long before he inherited the property outright, John Jay treated it like his own, maintaining gardens, planting trees, and establishing, in 1807, a tranquil cemetery lined with cypresses for himself, his siblings, and descendants. Together with his son Peter Augustus Jay, he oversaw the installation of gardens and elm tree plantings in Rye. He guided his son's introduction of stone ha-ha walls in 1822 as a means to frame not only the

20 *See* Jay Heritage Center website, *https://tclf.org/landslides/the-jay-property-threatened-by-erasure.*

landscape, but specifically the wide-open meadow that stretched to the water. The ha-ha walls served many functional as well as aesthetic purposes including: an uninterrupted view of the water from the Mansion; a formalized Palladian vista of the estate from the Long Island Sound; a means to keep livestock from straying off the property; and a way to conceal an irrigation system that connected wells to fields and gardens throughout the property.

* * *

> The most prominent feature of this landscape is an expansive meadow that is believed to be the oldest man-managed meadow on record in New York State. This magnificent swath of golden grass pre-dated [John Jay's] family's residency by thousands of years, to Paleo-Indian times when the land was a fertile settlement site and regularly burned to renew growth. John Jay and generations of Jays, including the slaves they owned and emancipated, were themselves stewards of this landscape that had been mapped out by primitive human hands and tools. Like the Siwanoys before them, the Jays used controlled fires to rejuvenate their fields and maintain these same vistas of the horizon.[21]

So, we may inquire whose legacy is society to celebrate at the childhood home of John Jay? The Jay Heritage Center will encounter a new category of challenges as its historic structures and landscape experience impacts associated with climate change.[22] To reflect all of John Jay's legacy, alliances will need to be made with other places that celebrate Jay, such as his *alma mater,* Columbia University in Manhattan, the Jay Homestead in Bedford, the New York Capital in Albany, and the State Department and Supreme Court in Washington, D.C. Jay's legacy is still fragmented. The Jay Heritage Center offers a home for integrating it. The debate over Jay's legacy is continuing.

---

21 Jay Heritage Center, "Stewardship Through Smart Choices", *https://jayheritagecenter.org/visit/buildings-grounds/stewardship-through-smart-choices.*

22 The Jay Property and climate change is discussed in Chapter 10e, infra.

CHAPTER 3:
FINDING MEANING THROUGH HISTORIC PRESERVATION

3A. STORIES TOLD THROUGH HISTORIC PRESERVATION

Historic preservation has come to mean identifying and keeping safe, the monuments of history and evolving civilization. The monuments enfolded within this enterprise are not just physical things, like buildings and bridges, but also places that were eventful, like battlegrounds and protests and places to be kept uneventful, like landscapes and burial grounds. These monuments are protected not simply because they are old, but especially because they tell a story—of living, of commerce, of strife, of discovery, of creativity, of wonder, of grief. The bullet-ridden buildings in Chicago are monuments to a troubling crime era of the 1920s, just as much as the Louis Sullivan skyscrapers remind us of the city's architectural vision. Highways, such as Route 66 (the Lincoln Highway) tell the stories of many small-towns and the things that brought and kept them together and of those traveling through to adventure. Monuments to our maritime heritage (the frigate Constitution—Old Ironsides, the 1877 square-rigger Elissa, the Intrepid) tell us how we made war and defended our shores. Old factories reveal the industrial imperatives of the times as they impacted the condition of the laborers. The Art Deco style is preserved in the Miami Beach Historic District as a tribute to historical antiquity. In Grand Teton National Park, long before it became a national park, there were homesteads, cattle operations and dude ranches. Places, prized natural objects or crafted buildings, artifacts, all cause us to remember what was, how we thought, what we revered and celebrated. They help us navigate the contemporary and to chart the future. Sometimes, as with John Jay's family home in Rye, we struggle to remember what is important. We choose to tell this story, to define or ascribe meaning, to the structures that we safeguard. What we save gives a sense of continuity. We preserve a "link between the time that was and the time that is. We look back even as we move forward."[1] Preserving reminds us that the present "civilization did not spring full-grown from the brow of Zeus."[2]

As suggested in the opening chapter to this book, preserving monuments is not without contention, given the property rights-focused society we live in. The regime of legal protections for historic areas or buildings is often seen as intruding upon the rights of the owners when it restricts the full exploitation of allowable development opportunities. There are those who believe that "ownership" and its concomitant stick in the bundle—the right to develop to the greatest extent possible to get the maximum return on their investment, should prevail even at the cost of our nation's heritage. This notion however was soundly rejected in *Penn Central Transp. Co. v. New York City*, where the Supreme Court stated that "structures with special historic, cultural, or architectural significance enhance the quality of life for all. Not only do these buildings and their workmanship represent the lessons of the past and embody precious features of our heritage, they serve as examples of quality for today."[3] Historic preservation regulations thus serve a higher public purpose, one that cities can use as a tool if they so choose in order to protect those places that give a community identity and those that are important to the cultural heritage of a city. Imagine New York City without the Empire State Building or Chicago without the Willis Tower (formerly the Sears Tower) or New Orleans without the Vieux Carré District. Historic preservation protects the things that remind us of happy times, like Mark Twain's house in Connecticut where he joked and frolicked with his children, and those that are chilling, like the Texas School Book Depository where Lee Harvey Oswald lay in wait to assassinate President John F. Kennedy, and those that are breathtaking, like the Grand Canyon.

3B. THE FORMAL ORIGINS OF HISTORIC PRESERVATION

The earliest organized efforts at preserving the historic concerned structures associated with revered persons and came in 1813 when a group of Philadelphians

1 T.H. Watkins, *Trust and Civilization: A Heritage Preserved*, 32 The Wilson Qtrly. Issue 5 (Aug/Sept 1981).

2 *Id.*

3 438 U.S. 104, 108 (1978).

blocked a sale and destruction of the city's Old State House, today known as Independence Hall. Then, in 1856 the Mt. Vernon Ladies' Association, organized and raised funds to preserve Mt. Vernon, George Washington's plantation in Mt. Vernon, Virginia. A codicil in the will of one of his heirs provided for the purchase of the plantation by Congress or the state of Virginia, but neither did and the estate fell into disrepair. The Mount Vernon's Ladies' Association launched a crusade to raise funds that eventually acquired the site. Around this time also, in 1850, the State of New York acquired George Washington's headquarters in Newburgh, New York, as the first historic site in the country acquired for its preservation by any government.[4] Public interest in preserving American history continued to grow. Beginning in 1890, the Daughters of the American Revolution expanded its reach in protecting Revolutionary War ideals, heroes, and historic places through a network of state and local affiliates. Financial assistance from the National Association of Colored Women in 1896 was instrumental in protecting Cedar Hill, Frederick Douglass' home in Washington, D.C.[5] In 1926, the Reverend William Goodwin persuaded John D. Rockefeller, Jr. to spend millions of dollars on the restoration of Colonial Williamsburg.[6]

In 1893, Congress enacted the Sundry Civil Appropriations Act that authorized the Secretary of War to spend not more than $25,000 for monuments and tablets identifying troop positions and movements at Gettysburg. When railroad construction threatened to divide this historic battlefield, Congress later authorized the Secretary of War to acquire land to protect this landscape permanently. The railroad challenged the use of eminent domain for the acquisition. The Supreme Court's reading of the government's eminent domain powers was expansive. In *U.S. v. Gettysburg Electric R. Co.*,[7] it declared protection of the lands of "one of the great battles of the world" a valid public purpose and thus, upheld the use of the condemnation power. Detailed rules regulating the placement of monuments

4 It was here that General Washington: (a) rejected the suggestion of an American monarchy; (b) ended the Newburgh Conspiracy, preventing potential military control of the government; (c) created the Badge of Military Merit, forerunner of the Purple Heart; (d) circulated an influential letter to State Governors outlining the key principles he felt necessary for the new republic; and (e) announced the Cessation of Hostilities, which ended the fighting of the Revolutionary War. See *https://parks.ny.gov/historic-sites/17/details.aspx.*

5 Frederick Douglass, National Historic Site, National Park Service, *https://home.nps.gov/frdo/learn/historyculture/preservation.htm.*

6 The History of Colonial Williamsburg, *https://www.history.org/Foundation/cwhistory.cfm.*

7 160 U.S. 668 (1896).

and markers, and establishing codes of conduct for visitors at Gettysburg and four other prominent Civil War battlefields, were promulgated by the Secretary of War in 1914.

Along with battlefield sites, archaeological sites were a matter of scientific interest as early as the 18th century. Congress chartered the Smithsonian Institution in 1846 "for the increase and diffusion of knowledge among men."[8] In 1879, the Archaeological Institute of America was founded. It is North America's oldest and largest organization devoted to the world of archaeology. It was created to "further[] and direct[] archaeological and artistic investigation and research."[9]

Until 1947, historic preservation was largely carried out by individual citizens and isolated organizations, small groups that focused on local projects. But these efforts were limited by their nature and scale—requiring adequate funds, large membership, and local investment. In 1949, Congress chartered the National Trust for Historic Preservation,[10] which brought preservation onto the national scene. The National Trust has a role in all aspects of historic preservation, from facilitating public participation in the preservation movement, educating the public, advising government agencies and private parties on standards for preservation, and managing the historic properties under its ownership.[11] In its early days, it acquired Woodlawn Plantation in Mt. Vernon, Virginia and Casa Amesti in Monterey, California.

The movement crystallized in 1966 with the release of the seminal report of the U.S. Conference of Mayors, Special Committee on Historic Preservation, with the Ford Foundation, WITH HERITAGE SO RICH.[12] The report was the culmination

---

8 20 U.S.C. §41.

9 The United States Congress issued the society a charter in 1906. The stated mission is "to promote archaeological inquiry and public understanding of the material record of the human past to foster an appreciation of diverse cultures and our shared humanity." It does this by providing support for archaeologists, their research and by encouraging the ethical practice of archaeology. *https://www.archaeological.org/about/history.*

10 A Brief History of the National Trust for Historic Preservation, *https://savingplaces.org/trust-history*; David E. Finley,& the Founding of the National Trust, Forum Journal & Forum Focus, *https://forum.savingplaces.org/viewdocument/david-e-finely-and-the-founding-of.*

11 *https://savingplaces.org/*

12 U.S. Conference of Mayors, Special Committee on Historic Preservation, WITH HERITAGE SO RICH (1966).

of meetings and discussions about the future of preservation, at a national conference co-sponsored by Colonial Williamsburg and the National Trust for Historic Preservation.[13] It recounted the state of historic monuments in the country, offering vivid images of large scale demolition by neglect and on purpose, of hundreds of historic buildings in every city—more than half of the historic structures listed in the WPA Historic American Buildings Survey ("HABS"). This very serious state of affairs was told vividly and movingly through an eclectic volume of essays, poetry, photography and policy statements. The report recommended the creation of an Advisory Council on Historic Preservation ("ACHP") to represent the paramount interests at all levels of government and the private sector and to serve as a liaison for the coordination of development and preservation efforts.[14] The work prompted deep thinking about what we were doing to preserve monuments and what we were doing to destroy them. That work, along with the efforts of the National Trust for Historic Preservation led to the passage of the National Historic Preservation Act of 1966 ("NHPA").[15] At the time, the National Trust declared "that the historic and cultural foundations of the Nation should be preserved as a living part of our community life and development in order to give a sense of orientation to the American people." The NHPA established the National Trust as the chief spokesperson and adviser on matters of historic preservation and authorized annual grants for its operations.[16]

When WITH HERITAGE SO RICH appeared, local governments had already taken the lead in preserving historic structures and places. The earliest local ordinance came from Charleston, South Carolina in 1931, when the city enacted the first historic district legislation. New Orleans, Louisiana followed suit. The Charleston ordinance has served to protect antebellum houses and cobblestone streets. In New Orleans, the Vieux Carré district preserves the Old French Quarter, the unique French styled architecture and brilliant palette of colors.

The demand to protect historic places emerged at the municipal, grass roots, level across the country. It was the creative and effective enactment of local ordinances to recognize and protect the public interest in the historic and

13 Forum Journal, Fall 2015, Vol. 30, No. 1 at 3.

14 WITH HERITAGE SO RICH at 192. The work of the ACHP is discussed further at Chapter 7.

15 54 U.S.C. §300101, *et seq.*, as amended.

16 *See David E. Finley, supra* note 10.

architectural importance of a structure, regardless of its ownership, that emboldened the New York City Council to enact its Landmarks Preservation Law. Other municipalities explored doing so as well, but often were held back worrying about whether their police powers extended to curbing some development plans of private property owners. This would change with the United States Supreme Court's endorsement of the New York City Landmarks Preservation Law in 1978, retold in the next chapter.[17]

By the mid-1970's, historic preservation had become a firmly embedded institution. The New York Times's architecture critic, Ada Louise Huxtable, marveled at how swiftly preservation had moved from "an odd and harmless hobby of little old ladies in floppy hats who liked old houses" into what she called "an integral, administrative part of city government dealing with an essential part of the city's fabric;" an "environmental necessity."[18]

17 The complete story of the judicial decisions supporting the New York City Landmarks Preservation Law is set forth in Nicholas A. Robinson and Shelby D. Green, Chapter 2, "Constitutional Foundations for Preservation," in Historic Preservation—Law And Culture (2018).

18 Ada Louise Huxtable, 'From Sentiment to Social Force," N.Y. Times, Feb. 3, 1974.

CHAPTER 4:
DESIGNATING AND PRESERVING A LANDMARK: THE STORY OF GRAND CENTRAL TERMINAL

4A. THE THEORY OF HISTORIC PRESERVATION

PENNSYLVANIA STATION AND GRAND CENTRAL TERMINAL

Pennsylvania Station New York City

Old Metropolitan Opera House

Grand Central Terminal

In 1963, the beautiful, natural light-filled beaux art Pennsylvania Station had been in service for only 53 years. It was designed by McKim, Mead and White and completed in 1910. But, when rail travel began to decline with the steady rise in automobile travel, the owners sought to convert the very valuable real estate on which the station was built into higher revenue generating activity. Despite strong public protest, the edifice was toppled, nothing was preserved; indeed, some of its artistically carved bas relief was later found dumped in wetlands across the Hudson River in the Meadowlands of New Jersey. Public protests went unheard. Where once travelers elegantly gathered to board their trains in the great halls inspired by the Roman Baths of Caracalla, since the 1960s, passengers dwelt underground, in a crowded, low-ceilinged, dimly-lit, cavern-like space. In place of the lost beauty, Madison Square Garden, a fairly non-descript urban building was put up. The garden is a venue for concerts and the home of the New York Knickerbockers basketball team. Unable to stop the wrecking of Pennsylvania Station and grieving at the demolition of the Metropolitan Opera House,[1] New York City took forward-looking action—it enacted the Landmarks Preservation Law in 1965.

Under the law, the Landmarks Preservation Commission, comprised of architects, historians, planners and business people, may designate as a landmark a nominated property that evinces "a special character or a special historical

1 The Metropolitan Opera House, also known as the "Old Met," was a large opera house in New York City. It was built in the early 1880s, in response to the desire by the new moneyed class for a facility befitting New York high society. This five-balcony auditorium housed 3389 people—with a design that attempted to meet the standards of European artists. It had five balconies and main floor, with box seating and space for 380 standees. Two tiers of boxes and a row of baignoires, together called the "Golden Horseshoe," were claimed by members of New York's high society, the Vanderbilts, Morgans, Goulds, and the other original seventy stockholders and were visually and physically separated them from the standees. The House was nicknamed "The Warehouse," and had a yellow-brick façade, in the Italian Renaissance style with Romanesque panels. The House featured world renowned works, conductors, and performers, including that of Wagner and Puccini and Toscanini and Caruso. Not long after construction, however, the House was thought to be inadequate, having been designed by someone who never before designed a theater and efforts to construct a new theater began. In the early to mid-1960s, attempts to demolish and replace the House to resolve functional issues were met with the multi-million dollar "Save the Met" historic preservation campaign. While then Secretary of the Interior Stewart Lee Udall had determined the Metropolitan Opera House eligible for National Historic Landmark designation in December 1962—and despite the best efforts of "Save the Met"—the Metropolitan Opera Association, Inc. declined Landmark designation on account of its plans to replace the opera house. At the same time, the New York City Landmarks Preservation Commission voted against designating the House as a city landmark. In 1967, the Old Met was demolished as part of the construction of the current Metropolitan Opera House in the Lincoln Center of Performing Arts, which had opened the previous year. *https://www.nps.gov/subjects/nationalhistoriclandmarks/metropolitan-opera-house.htm.*

or aesthetic interest or value, as part of the development, heritage or cultural characteristics of the city..." whose destruction and alterations would mean "the irreplaceable loss to the people of the city of the aesthetic, cultural and historic values represented by such improvements and landscape features."[2] One of the first structures so designated under the new law was Grand Central Terminal. The Commission's designation report made its findings supporting designation of the Terminal as a City landmark as follows:

> Grand Central Station, one of the great buildings of America, evokes a spirit that is unique in this City. It combines distinguished architecture with a brilliant engineering solution, wedded to one of the most fabulous railroad terminals of our time. Monumental in scale, this great building functions as well today as it did when built. In style it represents the best of the French Beaux Arts.
>
> The contrast of solids and voids is a striking feature of this building. The large percentage of glass areas, to be seen in the great windows, is reminiscent of the quality of some of the best French exposition buildings, models of daring structural design in their day, which availed themselves of the latest technological knowledge of their time. The use of these windows for several levels of horizontal circulation, was in itself a daring concept. Visitors can see from the main concourse the diminutive human beings walking between the two layers of glass as they cross and recross from office to office.
>
> The very scale of the monumental columns and the handsome sculptured details, such as the enframement of the oval windows and clock, represents a handsome and skillful combination of architectural elements to create a building overpowering in its timeless grandeur.
>
> **History of the Building**
>
> Superimposed upon the railroad empire built by the Vanderbilts, which in turn had been built upon the maritime empire of the old Commodore, was the vast network of rails soon to culminate in a new terminal

2 N.Y.C. Admin. Code § 25-301(a).

> destined to serve the greatest city in the country. On the shoulders of William J. Wilgus rested the staggering problem of assembling the fabulous network of electrified rails into this modern nerve center. This brilliant solution was approved to serve as the basic set of conditions for a nationwide competition among architects for the design of the terminal. The competition was won by Reed & Stem of St. Paul, Minnesota. It was their brilliant design which introduced the concept of ramps. Later Whitney Warren, of Warren & Wetmore, with the concurrence of the Vanderbilts, took over the architectural design of the terminal, as we see it today, displaying the virtuosity of his training at the Ecole des Beaux Arts in Paris.
>
> Grand Central always has been a symbol of the City itself. Commuters, sightseers, casual visitors and City dwellers on pleasant walks go through it daily. * * *[3]

In 1968, Penn Central Transportation Company, the then owners of Grand Central, filed an application with the Landmarks Preservation Commission to build a 55-story office tower atop the 1913 terminal. Penn Central presented alternative plans—one involved erecting a tower of glass and steel, unadorned, that would cantilever over the terminal (Breuer I) and another, the destruction of the terminal, saving only the grand concourse (Breuer II Revised). The justification for the height and density was the desire to benefit from the site's development rights above the terminal. At the public hearing on the request, there were scores on both sides. Noted figures against the proposal included Jacqueline Kennedy Onassis and Bess Myerson, former consumer advocate for New York City, architect Philip Johnson and Ed Koch, U.S. Congressman from New York. Surprisingly, the administrator of the Metropolitan Museum of Art, the director of the Whitney Museum and the editor of the Architectural Forum were in support. The public was not. In no uncertain terms, the Commission rejected the application for a "certificate of appropriateness" (COA") to carry out the plans, calling Breuer I an "aesthetic joke" and finding that the destruction of the exterior under Breuer II Revised was hardly consistent with the preservation of the structure. Penn Central sought review of the denial in the state courts and the trial court found that the Landmarks Commission's denial

3 Grand Central Terminal Landmark Designation Report, Landmarks Preservation Commission August 2, 1967, Number 2 LP-0266.

amounted to a confiscation of property rights, since Penn Central stood to lose lucrative leasing opportunities. Penn Central needed the wealth from the development in order to get it out of the dire financial straits it was in. The Landmarks Commission appealed, and the intermediate appellate court reversed the trial court, finding that Penn Central had failed to prove that it could not continue to use the terminal as a terminal and at a profit. The state's highest court, the Court of Appeals, affirmed. Agreeing with Penn Central that a landowner has an expectation of a reasonable return from his property, but finding that it wasn't just Penn Central's investment that was relevant to the calculus. Instead, much of the total value of the property had been contributed by the state—easements to lay the tracks, crossings, tax abatements, coordination of city subway with interstate rails. Penn Central had the burden of separating out these factors. The court also noted that Penn Central had usable transferable development rights,[4] that would enable some return on its investment.

Penn Central appealed the ruling to the U.S. Supreme Court, rehearsing the arguments made in the state court. The U.S. Supreme Court was not persuaded and affirmed in *Penn Central Transp. Co. v. New York City.*[5] The subject of historic preservation presented an occasion for adding nuances to the prevailing regulatory takings analysis. The Court laid out three factors: the economic impact of the regulation, the extent to which the regulation affects the landowner's distinct investment-backed expectations, and the character of the government actions. The Court first ruled that the city's "objective of preserving structures and areas with special historic, architectural, or cultural significance is an entirely permissible governmental goal."[6] It declared that states and cities may enact land use restrictions or controls to enhance the quality of life by preserving the character and desirable aesthetic features of the city.[7] Historic preservation laws, despite charges that they unconstitutionally burdened some landowners more than others, accord with law, because individual buildings had been designated in accordance with a comprehensive scheme for protecting historic resources. Unlike discriminatory zoning, the antithesis of land use control as part of some comprehensive plan, the New York City law embodied a comprehensive plan

4 Discussed at Chapter 5.

5 438 U.S. 104 (1978).

6 438 U.S. at 108.

7 *Id.* at 108.

to preserve structures of historic or aesthetic interest wherever they might be found in the city.[8]

In measuring the economic impact of the regulation, the Court adopted the "parcel as a whole" concept. This means that any diminution in value, must be measured with reference to the entire parcel, not just that which the regulation burdens. In this respect, the analysis must consider the value of what is retained. Grand Central Terminal comprises six city blocks and Penn Central retained valuable transferable development rights. As to Penn Central's investment-backed expectations, the Court found that the terminal could continue to be used for its original purposes. Even though the injunction to preserve the historic façade meant Penn Central could not build the proposed office tower of the building, the court made clear that mere diminution in property value as a consequence of land use regulation was not a taking *per se.*

With the constitutionality of preservation laws sustained by the Supreme Court, local governments proceeded to enact new ordinances patterned upon the New York City Law. Essentially, local governments would survey and study their buildings and sites, make a reasoned decision based on the study to designate landmarks after which the owner is obliged to apply for a "Certificate of Appropriateness" explaining how any proposed changes would maintain the historic character of the landmark. At each step of the process, the public has a right to share comments and be heard.

4B. HISTORIC LANDMARKS IN NEW YORK CITY

Since *Penn Central*, the New York City Landmarks Preservation Commission has gone on to designate roughly 40,000 buildings and a few hundred districts. Some are readily known, the Chrysler Building, Gracie Mansion, the Empire State Building, St. Patrick's Cathedral, the Apollo Theater, some more obscure, the Downtown Dutch Street Pattern, 359 Broadway (where the Photographer Mathew Brady had a studio), the Hopper-Gibbons House (used as a safe house

8 *Id.* at 132.

for fugitive slaves).[9] Across the City, neighborhoods whose buildings reflect design features of the same time period in which they were built, have been designated as historic districts, such as Brooklyn Heights. Local neighborhood organizations provide public participation in favor of the landmarks and districts in their area, such as the Greenwich Village Society for Historic Preservation. Citizen advocates for preservation law are essential partners with the preservation commissions in sustaining preservation laws.

Local preservation laws are best understood by the decisions that protect historical structures. Comparable dynamics are found regardless of whether the locally situated structures date from the 17th or 20th centuries—buildings at least 30 years old of the immediate past generation, can be deemed landmarks in New York City, whether the cities are as big as New York or small hamlets. Although the Supreme Court affirmed the validity of historic preservation laws, the act of designating structures is yet not without challenge and cities continue to landmark buildings against owners' objections.[10]

9 *See* Matt A.V. Chaban, *Landmark Status Is Urged for 30 New York City Properties,* N.Y. Times.(Feb. 23, 2016)(including the neon Pepsi sign on the Queens waterfront, the Bergdorf Goodman department store on Fifth Avenue and parts of the Green-Wood Cemetery in Brooklyn); *see also New York City Landmarks Law at 50, https://www.nytimes.com/2015/04/18/opinion/new-york-citys-landmarks-law-at-50.html#slideshow/100000003634679/100000003635262.*

10 *See e.g.,* Ben Brachfeld, *City Landmarks Brooklyn Home Against Owner's Wishes,* Gotham Gazette (March 02, 2018). In October 2017, the city's Landmarks Preservation Commission voted to designate the Peter P. and Rosa M. Huberty House, at 1019 Bushwick Avenue in Brooklyn, as a city landmark. The Commission stated: "The designation of the Huberty House honors both the historic character of Bushwick Avenue as it developed in the early 20th century, as well as the contributions of architect Ulrich Huberty to the borough of Brooklyn." LPC Chair Meenakshi Srinivasan said at the time, "Today's landmark designation will preserve this splendid Colonial Revival for future generations of New Yorkers to enjoy." *See also* Jonathan Wolfe, *Landmark Status for Corcoran Gallery of Art Interior,* N.Y. Times, April 24, 2015 (reporting on the designation of the interior of the Corcoran Art Gallery over the objections of the building's owner, George Washington University). The case of the Strand Bookstore is discussed below.

4C. THE MECHANICS OF HISTORIC PRESERVATION

THE VICTORIAN COTTAGE IN VIEUX CARRÉ, NEW ORLEANS

Vieux Carré

Beginning in 1963, Maher, sought to demolish his Victorian styled cottage and to erect in its place a seven-apartment complex. The cottage was located in the Vieux Carré Historic District of New Orleans. Organizations and property owners united to oppose the plan. After many requests, Maher won the Historical Commission's consent, but the City Council overruled the commission and forbade the grant of a demolition permit.

As a background to the dispute, the Louisiana Constitution was amended in 1936 to vest in the City of New Orleans the power to create a Commission whose purpose was stated to be:

> The preservation of such buildings in the Vieux Carré section of the City of New Orleans as, in the opinion of said Commission, shall be deemed to have architectural and historical value, and which buildings should be preserved for the benefit of the people of the City of New Orleans and the State of Louisiana, and to that end the Commission shall be given

> such powers and duties as the ... City of New Orleans shall deem fit and necessary.[11]

To implement the historic preservation plan, the City enacted the Vieux Carré Ordinance, which established the Vieux Carré Commission and created a framework of rules governing its powers, duties and operations. The Ordinance required that proposals for any alteration or demolition work within the District be submitted to the Commission, accompanied by the full plans and specifications as they relate to the proposed appearance, color, texture of materials and architectural design of the exterior, including the front, sides, rear and roofs of buildings in the district and for alterations or additions of any outbuilding, party wall, courtyard, or fence.[12]

Maher brought suit first in state court seeking a declaration that the City Council's action was outside its statutory authority. While prevailing in the trial court, Maher lost the next two rounds in the state appellate courts. The case was ultimately decided by the United States Court of Appeals for the Fifth Circuit, in *Maher v. New Orleans.*[13] Maher's challenge was one of substantive due process; specifically, that although the legislative purpose underlying the preservation of the Vieux Carré District was unobjectionable, its enforcement was arbitrary in that it lacked adequate standards. Moreover, because the ordinance precluded other beneficial uses of the property, it amounted to a taking that required compensation.

SUPREME COURT PRECEDENT

This case was decided before *Penn Central* which articulated a "test" for regulatory takings. But, there was a long history of Supreme Court cases affirming that land use regulations carry a presumption of constitutionality.[14] The court

11 La. Const. Art. XIV, Sec. 22A. The same section further charges the Commission with assuring "that the quaint and distinctive character of the Vieux Carré section of the City of New Orleans may not be injuriously affected, ... that the value to the community of those buildings having architectural and historical worth may not be impaired, and . . that a reasonable degree of control may be exercised over the architecture of [buildings in] said Vieux Carré section ...."

12 Vieux Carré Ordinance § 65-8 (submission of plans for exterior changes to Commission).

13 516 F.2d 1051 (5th Cir. 1975), *cert. denied,* 426 U.S. 905 (1976).

14 *Goldblatt v. Hempstead,* 369 U.S. 590 (1962); *Village of Euclid v. Ambler Realty Co.,* 272 U.S. 365 (1926).

read these cases to say that this was true, so long as the regulation is "within the perimeter of the police power, an authority residing in the law-making body to secure, preserve and promote the general health, welfare and safety."[15] This meant that a regulatory ordinance that bears a real and substantial relation to a legitimate state purpose, where the means selected are reasonable and of general application, and does not trench impermissibly on other constitutionally protected interests, will be upheld.[16] In identifying a legitimate public interest and purpose, courts will generally defer to legislative bodies, who are generally entrusted with the task of enacting laws in furtherance of the general good. While the police power is not unlimited, its boundaries are both ample and protean; proper state purposes may encompass not only the goal of abating undesirable conditions, but of fostering ends the community deems worthy. The court noted *Berman v. Parker*, in which the Supreme Court, giving "well-nigh conclusive" effect to the legislative determination of community needs and solutions, upheld the purposes of a slum clearance program designed to "develop a more balanced, more attractive community."[17] In this respect, the values advanced need not be solely economic or directed at health and safety in their narrowest senses, but can encompass more generous, subtle and intangible societal interests—"[t]he values [the police power] represent are spiritual as well as physical, aesthetic as well as monetary. It is within the domain of the legislature to determine that the community should be beautiful as well as healthy, spacious as well as clean, well-balanced as well as carefully patrolled."[18]

The court found *Village of Euclid v. Ambler Realty Co.*, as "the watershed case upholding the right of a municipality to enact a general zoning ordinance." There, the Supreme Court observed:

> Problems have developed, and constantly are developing, which require, and will continue to require, additional restrictions in respect of the use and occupation of private lands in urban communities. Regulations, the wisdom, necessity and validity of which, as applied to existing conditions,

15 516 F.2d at 1058.

16 516 F.2d at 1059.

17 348 U.S. 26 (1954). *See also Village of Belle Terre v. Boraas*, 416 U.S. 1 (1974) ("the police power is not confined to elimination of filth, stench and unhealthy places. It is ample to lay out zones where family values ... and the blessings of quiet seclusion ... make the area a sanctuary for people.").

18 *Id.* at 33.

> are so apparent that they are now uniformly sustained, a century ago, or even half a century ago, probably would have been rejected as arbitrary and oppressive.[19]

PURPOSES OF THE VIEUX CARRÉ ORDINANCE

Given these guideposts, the court had little trouble upholding the New Orleans ordinance, first pointing to the declared objective:

> The Vieux Carré shall have for its purpose the preservation of such buildings in the Vieux Carré section of the City as, in the opinion of the Commission, shall have architectural and historical value and which should be preserved for the benefit of the people of the City and State.[20]

The court found that the Vieux Carré Ordinance furthered the object of preserving the character of the district in a meaningful fashion. It applied to a well-defined geographic area. The law would be administered by a Commission whose professional qualifications and means of selection were delineated. Within the boundaries of the French Quarter, the Commission was directed to review plans for all proposed demolition or construction under well-defined procedures. There was review of the Commission's decision by the City Council.[21]

GUIDANCE IN THE ORDINANCE

There were ample provisions in the ordinance to prevent any arbitrary application; the first being the state constitution stating the general goal[22] and the ordinance incorporated this goal—to protect structures with particular historic

19 272 U.S. at 386-87.

20 Vieux Carré Ordinance § 65-6. In addition to conferring cultural benefits, it was not contested that preservation of the Vieux Carré district promoted the economic welfare of the city by attracting tourists.

21 Vieux Carré Ordinance §§ 65-5; -8 to -10.

22 La. Const. Art. XIV, § 22A, allows the City to protect "the quaint and distinctive character of the area."

and architectural merit,[23] into its provisions. The ordinance delineated the district,[24] defined what alterations in which locations required approval,[25] and contained guidelines for items of special interest, such as floodlights, overhanging balconies or signs.[26] Moreover, the ordinance specified the composition of the Commission (required to include architects, historians and business persons offering complementary skills, experience and interests) to ensure knowledgeable decision-making.[27] The elaborate appeal process created another structural check on any potential for arbitrariness.[28] The court explained that "[t]o satisfy due process, guidelines to aid a commission charged with implementing a public zoning purpose need not be so rigidly drawn as to prejudge the outcome in each case, precluding reasonable administrative discretion."[29]

NOT A TAKING

Finally, the court rejected the takings claim, noting that the Supreme Court repeatedly had made clear that an ordinance within the police power does not become an unconstitutional taking merely because, as a result of its operation, property does not achieve its maximum economic potential. The court, however, cautioned that there may be circumstances where the expense of maintenance under the Ordinance could be so unreasonable as to constitute a taking, but that the burden of proving such a case falls on the party alleging the taking. On the evidence presented, the court was constrained to defer to the district court which found that Maher had not sustained his burden.[30] By this expansive explication of the powers of local government to determine the permissible character and development within its borders, the cottage was thus saved and local historic preservation law planted on firm ground.

---

23 Vieux Carré Ordinance § 65-6 charges the Commission to "preserv[e] such buildings ... [as] shall have architectural and historical value and which should be preserved for the benefit of the people..."

24 Vieux Carré Ordinance § 65-6.

25 Vieux Carré Ordinance § 65-8 (Ordinance extends to exterior work on any building that fronts on a public street or alley within the Vieux Carré).

26 Vieux Carré Ordinance §§ 56-11; -13; -17 to -33.

27 *Id.*

28 Vieux Carré Ordinance §§ 65-5; -8 to -10.

29 *Id.*

30 *Maher v. New Orleans,* 371 F. Supp. at 662.

Two cases from the Louisiana state courts that pre-date *Maher* are good illustrations of how the courts expounded upon the goals of historic preservation and how the Vieux Carré ordinance applied to achieve them. In *City of New Orleans v. Pergament*,[31] the court upheld the ordinance against a challenge to a section that prohibited a proprietor of any building in the district to maintain a display sign, or advertising sign, without first obtaining a permit from the Vieux Carré Commission. The ordinance prescribed the maximum size and the details of the various kinds of advertising signs which could be displayed. The maximum area of any sign or signboard allowed to be displayed in the Vieux Carré, was 8 square feet if only one side or surface of the sign was displayed, or 16 square feet if both sides are displayed. The defendant, who operated a gas station displayed a sign that had an area of 560 square feet. The lower part of the sign measured 24 feet in width and 20 feet in height, above which was an extension 12 feet wide and having an area of 80 square feet. The court ruled that the ordinance might be deemed violative of the equal protection clause in the Fourteenth Amendment if it undertook to confer upon the Vieux Carré Commission the authority to grant or withhold permits arbitrarily, or without prescribing uniform requirements or standards which all persons similarly situated should be obliged to comply with. But that was not the nature of the ordinance here. Finding the purpose of the ordinance was not only to preserve the old buildings themselves, but to preserve the antiquity of the whole French and Spanish quarter, the *tout ensemble*, the prohibition was within the police power and within the scope of this municipal ordinance. The preservation of the Vieux Carré as it was originally is a benefit to the inhabitants of New Orleans generally, not only for the sentimental value of the area, but for its commercial value as well.

In *City of New Orleans v. Impastato*,[32] the court interpreted the ordinance to apply to changes to be made to the exterior, even to the rear, of any building situated in the Vieux Carré section which fronts on a public street. In the court's reading, the word "exterior," clearly means all of the outer surfaces, as distinguished from the interior or the portion enclosed by the outer surfaces and cannot be limited to include only the front portion of the building. Such a strained interpretation of the language used in the constitutional amendment would merely serve to defeat the obvious intention of the people as expressed thereby rendering it

31 198 La. 852, 5 So.2d 129 (1941).

32 198 La. 206, 3 So.2d 559 (1941).

impossible for the Commission to preserve the architectural design of the sides, rear and roof of any building in the Vieux Carré section.

These three cases illustrate the importance of a comprehensive preservation plan, also the willingness of courts to carefully interpret the language toward the broad aims of the expressed policy.

4c1. WHAT TO DESIGNATE AS HISTORIC

A persistent dialogue and contention concerns the issue of the best criteria for determining what to preserve; what values are worthy and to whom are these important. Preservation can be burdensome—the owner is not allowed to change the character-defining traits (and this means no destruction) without approval by some commission and must maintain the property in its historic guise. Landowners resist designations, some preemptively demolish historic structures. The White House shrinks national monuments (Bears Ears and Grand Staircase Escalante)[33] and violate the terms of others (Mohave water pipeline).[34] The NHPA includes no substantive protections for those things on the National Register and individual listing is subject to an owners' veto. The tally of winners and losers does not clearly favor preservation, and any win does not seem to deter more challenges and violations.

The early preservation efforts focused on the physical things—mostly buildings, whose underlying values were associated primarily with western-oriented traditions or early national heroes. This might be explained somewhat by who the early preservationists were—upper middle-class individuals, who had the leisure and means to devote themselves to non-paying endeavors. Except in a few cities, until the NHPA, preservation meant saving the odd building threatened with destruction by development or deterioration (Mt. Vernon and Frederick

33 Discussed below.

34 On June 21, 2019, a federal court ruled that the Trump administration violated the law when it authorized plans to construct a 43-mile-long pipeline through Mojave Trails National Monument and other public land in southern California. The pipeline is part of the Cadiz water project, which would pump 16 billion gallons of water a year from the fragile desert aquifer to sprawling developments in Southern California. The court ruled that the railroad easements can be used only for activities that further a railroad purpose and the Trump administration failed to justify that the Cadiz pipeline serves that purpose. Federal Court Rejects Trump Administration's Approval Of California's Cadiz Water Pipeline, *https://earthjustice.org/news/press/2019/federal-court-rejects-trump-administration-s-approval-of-california-s-cadiz-water-pipeline*

Douglass' home); there was no forward-looking preservation philosophy. The NHPA pronounced the national policy that historic preservation was essential to our posterity and to the enhancement of the daily lives of people in communities. Although the criteria for listing on the National Register seem rather broad (association with a person, event, architecture or likely to generate important information),[35] the focus has traditionally been on material culture, that represented by buildings, districts, and landscapes. This has seemingly left out of our appreciation, the larger set of intangible social and environmental values that reside in these tangible things. It is only recently that preservation has broadened to cover *both* physical and intangible cultural heritage and to be more inclusive of its diversity. Monuments are being declared that celebrate movements (the Harriet Tubman Underground Railroad National Monument)[36], indigenous rituals (the Meteorite in the Museum of Natural History),[37] and community life (the Gullahs in South Carolina).[38] Heritage is now being linked, not so much to buildings, but to places of natural or cultural significance, and to embrace values that transcend the physical attributes of a structure.

Who decides whose history is important? Are the criteria reliable, fair and honest? Or does designation often turn on how good a narrative is made of the historical and cultural values and the individual predilections of the those deciding on the nomination. While it might be easier to mark values in terms of historic styles or a known person, much may be lost if we fail to consider intangible attributes such as the stance of a landscape, what inspired it and what it inspired. As architecture, history and art evolve, by what standards do we note and protect their "value." Or, is it that only ancient property is worthy of preservation? Is society still interested in quaintness or is accessibility, convenience,

35 The criteria are discussed further in Chapter 7.

36 *https://obamawhitehouse.archives.gov/the-press-office/2013/03/25/presidentialproclamation-harriet-tubman-underground-railroad-national-m.*

37 Discussed below at Chapter 7.

38 Katherine Schulz Richard, *The Gullah or Geechee Community of South Carolina and Georgia, https://www.thoughtco.com/the-gullah-language-1434488* (April 10, 2019). The Gullah people, also known as the Geechee are descended from African slaves who were recognized for their ability to grow crucial crops such as rice. Because the community was situated on islands off the coast of South Carolina and Georgia, the culture was largely isolated from white society and from other slave societies. They have preserved many of their African traditions and language elements. Some 250,000 people speak the Gullah language, a mixture of African words and the English that was spoken when slavery existed. The National Park Service oversees the Gullah/Geechee Cultural Heritage Corridor. A Gullah Museum exists on Hilton Head Island.

sustainability, and comfort equally important?[39] Is preservation still relevant to modern life? Is alternative documentation (photos, narratives, blueprints enough? Is virtual reality, by digitalization, just as good?[40]

What is the role and impact of New Urbanism? Should the budget-friendly bigbox stores (Wal-Mart, K-Mart, CVS, Target) be banned in order to preserve architecturally appealing central city buildings? While the central city and its older buildings and neighborhoods are clearly important, both to those who live there and to the larger community, so too are the post–World War II suburbs. While having commissions comprised of experts of history and architecture (ala *Maher*) go far to avoid idiosyncratic designations, would the process of designation be improved by having one or two neighbors or school teachers on the Commissions?

4C2. GUIDING HISTORIC DESIGNATION AT THE STATE LEVEL

As their local governments expand historic property regulation, states have expanded their state-wide statutes on historic preservation.[41] All states have enacted historic preservation acts that authorize their local governments to enact local historic preservation ordinances and regulate historic structures,[42]

39 *See* Margaret Jane Wyszomirski, "Policy Communities and Policy Influence: Securing a Government Role in Cultural Policy for the Twenty-First Century" in Gigi Bradford, Michael Gary, and Glenn Wallach, eds., *The Politics of Culture: Policy Perspectives for Individuals, Institutions, and Communities* (New York: New Press, 94-107 (2000)(addressing national arts policies and historic preservation).

40 In 2013, the European Union under the FP7 PEOPLE research framework, funded the "Initial Training Network for Digital Cultural Heritage ("CH"): Projecting our Past to the Future" with acronym ITN-DCH. It was the first and one of the largest Marie Curie fellowship projects in the area of the e-documentation/e-preservation and CH protection funded by the European Union. The project aimed to train 20 fellows in the area of CH digital documentation, preservation and protection. CH is touted as "an integral element of Europe and vital for the creation of a common European identity and one of the greatest assets for steering Europe's social, economic development and job creation." ITN-DCH will cover all aspects of CH ranging from the tangible (books, newspapers, images, drawings, manuscripts, uniforms, maps, artefacts, archaeological sites, monuments) to intangible content (e.g., music, performing arts, folklore, theatrical performances) and their inter-relationships. *Marie Curie Initial Training Network on Digital Cultural Heritage*, available on DocPlayer, *http://docplayer.net/47994142-Marie-curie-initial-training-network-on-digital-cultural-heritage-our-story.html.*

41 *See* e.g., N.Y.S. Office of Parks Recreation and Historic Preservation, *https://parks.ny.gov/shpo/.*

42 *See* e.g., New York Parks Rec. & His. Preserv. Law.

and many also regularly adopt long-term preservation plans.[43] Each state maintains a state historic preservation officer ("SHPO"), whose main function is to link the State to federal inventories of historic sites through the National Historic Preservation Act, by nominating properties for the National Register of Historic Places, and to consult in the case of undertakings that pose an adverse effect on properties on that register or eligible for listing, and to certify properties for federal and state historic tax credits.[44]

This pattern is illustrated by the New York State Historic Preservation Act of 1980,[45] which is a counterpart to the National Historic Preservation Act and declares historic preservation as an important state policy. The NYSHPA established the New York State Register of Historic Places, to inventory sites, buildings, structures, areas or objects significant in the history, architecture, archeology or culture of the state and local governments. The NYSHPA requires all state agencies to consult with the New York SHPO if state actions may change or impact the quality of any historic, architectural, archeological or cultural property that is listed on the National Register of Historic Places or listed on the State Register or *that is determined to be eligible for listing on the State Register.*[46] The NYSHPA requires state agencies, *to the fullest extent practicable*, to avoid or mitigate adverse impacts to such properties, to explore all feasible and prudent alternatives and to give due consideration to feasible and prudent plans that would avoid or mitigate adverse impacts to such property. All state agencies are required to designate a preservation officer to cooperate with the SHPO in implementing these obligations. The New York statute expanded the roles of a pre-existing State Board for Historic Preservation, which advises on statewide preservation planning efforts.[47] State legislation must co-exist with

---

43 Washington State, Department of Archeology and Historic Preservation, *https://dahp.wa.gov/project-review/preservation-laws*; New York State Historic Preservation Plan 2015-2020, *www.nysparks.com/shpo.*
For a comprehensive list of historic preservation programs among the states, *see* Georgetown University Historic Preservation Resources, National, *https://repository.library.georgetown.edu/handle/10822/761776.*

44 Advisory Council on Historic Preservation, *Preserving America's Heritage, An Overview of the National Historic Preservation Act and Historic Preservation* at 3.

45 N.Y. Parks Rec. & His. Preserv. L, art. 13-19.

46 See *https://parks.ny.gov/historic-preservation/bhs/documents/NYFieldServiceBrochure.pdf.*

47 *Id.*

other state duties. Some states, like Hawaii, protect both tangible and intangible cultural heritage of indigenous citizens.[48]

48 Hawaii Constitution, Art. XII, §7.

CHAPTER 5: HISTORIC PRESERVATION IN ACTION

5A. TYPES OF HISTORIC PRESERVATION ORDINANCES

The work of preserving privately owned buildings and structures largely takes place on the local level, through ordinances that provide for the designation of landmarks and the creation of historic districts. More than 2500 municipalities have adopted historic preservation ordinances, most pursuant to an express delegation of power from the state legislatures.[1] The ordinances are variously administered by boards or commissions, whose actions are either binding or advisory. There are many common features in the ordinances. First, there is a declaration of the importance of preserving monuments. There is often some mention of the improvement of the quality of our aesthetic lives. Others mention the importance of economic viability by preserving vibrant, eclectic and connected communities. The ordinances describe the criteria for landmarking, such as having "historical, architectural, archaeological, or cultural" value. The Charleston, South Carolina Ordinance provides:

> In order to promote the economic and general welfare of the city and of the public generally, and to insure the harmonious, orderly and efficient growth and development of the municipality, it is deemed essential by the city council of the city that the qualities relating to the history of the city and a harmonious outward appearance of structures which preserve property values and attract tourist and residents alike be preserved; some of these qualities being the continued existence and preservation of historic areas and buildings; continued construction of buildings in the

1 *See e.g.*, N.C. Gen. Stat. §§160A-400.1-400.14 (allowing local governments to create historic preservation commissions and to designate local historic districts and landmarks). In the statute, the General Assembly sets forth its finding that, "The historical heritage of our State is one of our most valued and important assets. The conservation and preservation of historic districts and landmarks stabilize and increase property values in their areas and strengthen the overall economy of the State."

> historic styles and a general harmony as to style, form, color, proportion, texture and material between buildings of historic design and those of more modern design; that such purpose is advanced through the preservation and protection of the old historic or architecturally worthy structures and quaint neighborhoods which impart a distinct aspect to the city and which serve as visible reminders of the historical and cultural heritage of the city, the state, and the nation.[2]

The Denver Landmark Preservation Law,[3] states: "It is hereby declared as a matter of public policy that the protection, enhancement, perpetuation and use of structures and districts of historical, architectural or geographic significance, located within the city or its mountain parks, is a public necessity, and is required in the interest of the prosperity, civic pride and general welfare of the people." The New York City Landmarks Preservation Law states the aim is to "foster civic pride in the beauty and noble accomplishments of the past." It does this by designating as historic landmarks, properties "having a special character or a special historical or aesthetic interest or value, as part of the development, heritage, or cultural characteristics of the city..."[4]

5B. ADMINISTRATION OF ORDINANCES

The Certified Governments Program, under the National Park Service, has promulgated a model preservation ordinance.[5] The model ordinance proposes a choice of models. One such as under the New York City Landmarks Preservation Law, where the Commission has the power to landmark a structure and another, under which a commission makes findings and recommendations for landmarking to a town board or council.[6]

---

2 Code of Ordinances, Sec. 54-230.

3 Code of Ordinance, ch. 30, Sec. 30-1.

4 N.Y. City Admin. Code §25-301(a).

5 *https://www.nps.gov/clg/.*

6 See Town of Greenburgh, N.Y. Historic Districts and Landmarks, Ch. 235, *https://ecode360.com/6816751.*

The New York City Landmarks Preservation Law,[7] is administered by a Commission, whose members consist of persons with a diverse array of expertise, including history, architecture, art, as well as real estate business.[8] Under the act, anyone can nominate a structure for designation as a local historic landmark. After nomination, the Commission conducts extensive research to verify the historic merits of the property. If the Commission decides to go forward, a public hearing is held. A majority vote of the Commission determines landmarking, but the city council must approve the Commission's decision.[9]

Ordinances protect historic property or landmarks of a certain age—in New York, at least 30 years old—first by designation, then by regulating alterations and demolitions. Local ordinances protect the exteriors of historic buildings, some interiors that are open to the public, as well as groups of properties, that is, historic districts.[10] Each of these will be discussed in turn below.

5C. LIMITS AND DUTIES AFTER DESIGNATION

After a property has been designated as an historic landmark, the owner becomes subject to specific duties and limitations. First, an owner must maintain the structure—make reasonable efforts to preserve the historic attributes. Most ordinances contain provisions for the imposition of penalties and fines in order to ensure that the property does not fall into a state of disrepair, such that it must be demolished.

An owner is not permitted to make any alterations to any character-defining attribute of the structure (historic windows, siding, roof line), nor demolish it, without first obtaining a certificate of appropriateness ("COA") from the Commission or Board. In *Penn Central*, the owners sought either to build a

7 N.Y. City Admin. Code §25-301.

8 N.Y. City Charter, Ch. 74, Landmarks Preservation Commission §3020.

9 N.Y. City Admin. Code §25-303(g)(1).

10 For example, in New York City, there are nearly 40,000 landmarks and more than 142 historic districts. *https://www1.nyc.gov/site/lpc/about/about-lpc.page.*

fifty-story office tower atop the Grand Central Terminal or to demolish it completely, neither of which earned a COA.[11]

Some ordinances provide accessible guidance for owners as to what sorts of changes require a COA, what kinds of changes may be allowed without first seeking a COA, what kinds of materials are acceptable.[12] While this limitation seems to be the most contentious between owners and commissions, it seems that the ordinances that contain the most instruction and are most flexible to owners are the ones that achieve the best results.[13]

5D. NON-PROFIT OWNERS

SAILORS' SNUG HARBOR

Sailors' Snug Harbor

11 The local preservation commission has great leeway in approving requests for alterations. *See e.g.*, David W. Dunlap, *Landmarks Group Approves Bold Plan for Hearst Building*, N.Y. Times, Nov. 28, 2001, reporting that the New York City Landmarks Preservation Commission approved an architectural plan that would permit the Hearst Corporation to complete the mid-Manhattan headquarters it began building 74 years ago, by constructing 36 floors atop the landmark six-story headquarters. The base of the building would be turned into an atrium up to 70 feet high, with views through skylights to the tower above, although it was not clear just how much of this would be open to the public.

12 *See e.g.*, Denver Code of Ordinances, §30-47 (design guidelines).

13 *See* Tad Heuer, *Living History: How Homeowners in a New Local Historic District Negotiate Their Legal Obligations*, 116 Yale L. J. 768 (2006-2007)(recounting the difficulties of owners to comply with historic district regulations on account of the absence of published guidance on permissible alterations; the burdens of application fees and the apparent lack of solicitude by the commission for modest income homeowners).

While the treatment, preservation, and regulation of properties in private ownership is settled, courts have had to fashion alternative standards for historic properties owned by non-profit entities. This is illustrated by the case of Sailors' Snug Harbor, which was located along the north shore of Staten Island, New York, near the ferry. The institution was originally built as a home for retired sailors, on land devised by Captain Robert Richard Randall, to be used for "aged, decrepit and worn-out seamen." At the time of his death, Randall's estate was located in a part of New York City that was then rural, but soon became developed. The institution was then relocated to Staten Island in 1831. The many buildings reflected an array of architectural styles from Greek Revival to Romantic Anglo-Italian. In the 1960s, when the Trustees of Snug Harbor considered demolishing the buildings and upgrading and modernizing the facilities, the New York City Landmarks Preservation Commission moved to designate six of the structures as historic landmarks. The six buildings designated were among the first twenty sites to be designated by the Commission. The designation was limited by a one-year grace period for the buildings that gave the Commission time to devise an alternative plan for them.

After designation, the Commission denied a COA to the Trustees to demolish the buildings, finding that the Trustees had not shown that razing the structures (as opposed to renovating) was the only way to achieve improvements in the housing for its residents.

The Trustees sued to undo the designation and challenged the regulation by the Commission on the ground that it would interfere with the property's profitability, arguing that the designated dormitories were functionally obsolete and the forced preservation of the buildings would keep Sailors' Snug Harbor from carrying out its charitable purpose: providing housing to retired sailors. They maintained that the "burden of designation" on the owner "outweighed any public benefit." The trial court agreed and in March 1967 ruled that the designation constituted an "unlawful taking of property without just compensation." An intermediate appellate court in *In the Matter of the Trustees of the Sailors' Snug Harbor in the City of New York v. Platt*,[14] reversed. The court ruled that the regulation might constitute an unlawful taking if its application posed an unreasonable hardship, but the test for making this determination was whether the

14 288 N.Y.S.2d 314 (N.Y. App. Div. 1968).

maintenance of the landmark either physically or financially prevents or seriously interferes with carrying out the charitable purpose. There was no showing here on whether the preservation of these buildings would seriously interfere with the use of the property, whether the buildings were capable of conversion to a useful purpose without excessive cost, or whether the cost of maintaining them would entail serious expenditure—all in the light of the purposes and resources of the petitioner. The case was remanded.

Efforts to sell the property were blocked by the Commission, until then Mayor John Lindsey orchestrated a sale of the six designated buildings to the city in February 2, 1971 for use as the Staten Island Museum. Sixty-five acres of the campus were sold to a developer and the City of New York purchased 15.4 acres in September 1973 for $1.8 million. The Sailors' home was relocated to North Carolina. The mid-1970s fiscal crisis slowed the creation of the museum, but a visit in July 1976 by Jacqueline Kennedy Onassis, on behalf of the Municipal Art Society, generated publicity for Sailors' Snug Harbor. In 1976, restoration work to transform the home into the Snug Harbor Cultural Center began and in 1984, renovation of the buildings by William A. Hall Associates was planned. In 1992, Jan Hird Pokorny was hired to perform a $1.7 million restoration of buildings that became part of the Snug Harbor Cultural Center.[15]

5E. ECONOMIC FEASIBILITY

The question whether the mere designation of a property as historic is a taking was settled by the Supreme Court in *Penn Central*. It is not a *per se* taking merely because the designation may not prohibit changes that would facilitate other uses. This is so because designation does not change the use of the historic structure, but only prohibits changes to the character-defining attributes without approval. In *Penn Central*, the railroad station could continue to be used after designation for the same purposes as it had been before designation. It is only when an owner proposes changes, that economic feasibility comes into play. In *Casey v. Mayor of Rockville*,[16] the Maryland Court of Appeals made this point

15 New York Preservation Archive Project, *http://www.nypap.org/preservation-history/sailors-snug-harbor/*.

16 929 A.2d 74 (Md. 2007).

clear when it ruled that the Historic Preservation Commission is not required to consider the economic infeasibility of preservation when deciding whether to designate a property as historic. Under the code,[17] a local body must consider whether the subject property had historical, archaeological, or architectural significance. It is only after the property is designated historic and a development permit application is filed that the statutory scheme[18] requires that economic feasibility and financial hardship be considered in determining whether a permit should be issued. Failing to consider economic impact is not a denial of due process where the landowner is given a full and fair hearing on the issue of the historical/architectural significance of the property, and there is an opportunity to present evidence regarding economic feasibility in connection with a later application to alter or demolish the property.[19]

5F. HARDSHIP

Most historic preservation ordinances contain a process and standards for evaluating economic hardship claims. These provisions serve as a safety valve where the burdens of preserving a property appear onerous. The measure of economic hardship varies among ordinances and for the type of property. Some make reference to the income status of the owner.[20] Under the New York City Landmarks Preservation Law, economic hardship exists if the owner is unable to realize a six percent return on the property.[21] This measure is obviously inappropriate for not-for-profit owners. In these cases, economic hardship is shown if the ordinance operates in a way to make it impossible for the owner to carry out organizational purposes.[22] In other municipalities, economic hardship requires

17 Md. Ann. Code art. 66B, § 8.02.

18 Md. Ann. Code art. 66B, §§ 8.06(b), 8.09, and 8.10.

19 929 A. 2d at 111.

20 D.C. Code § 6-1104(g); D.C. Code §1102(14)(providing exemptions for property owned by low-income persons).

21 N.Y. City Admin. Code § 25-309, 302(v).

22 *In the Matter of the Trustees of the Sailors' Snug Harbor,* 288 N.Y.S. 2d at 316. Even in cases of not-for-profit organizations, the courts often press the organizations to ensure that the only alternative is demolition. *See Rector, Wardens, & Members of Vestry of St. Batholomew's Church,* 914 F.2d 348 (2d Cir. 1990)(where the court pressed the landowner to demonstrate that a less destructive design or borrowing from its endowment to renovate the building was not feasible).

a showing that the ordinance leaves the property with no economic value or no reasonable economic return.[23] But, if there is a *reasonable* alternative economic use for the property after the imposition of the restriction on that property, there is no taking.[24] In no case, do the ordinances require that an owner be allowed to realize the highest and best use of the property. That issue was settled in *Penn Central.* The ordinances typically explain the process for obtaining a hardship finding and spell out what information the commission needs to evaluate hardship claims. The timing for reviewing hardship claims is also important. Such claims should be considered only after an application for approval to alter or demolish a structure has been denied, not while properties are still being considered for historic designation or before applications for alterations are acted upon. In effect, economic hardship review is comparable to the variance process under zoning laws.

In *Zaruba v. Village of Oak Park,*[25] the court rejected a claim of economic hardship that was apparently self-created or where the proposed alteration would not produce a greater economic return than maintaining the renovated structure.

5G. DEMOLITION AND DELAY

THE ITALIAN EMBASSY

The Italian Embassy

23 *Kalorama Heights Ltd. Partnership v. District of Columbia Dep't of Consumer & Regulatory Affairs,* 655 A.2d 865 (D.C. Ct. App. 1995).

24 *Id.*

25 695 N.E.2d 510 (Ill. Ct. App. 1998)(owner bought severely dilapidated property in historic district and failed to show that demolition produced a smaller economic loss than rehabilitation and resale).

Stark choices confront Landmarks Preservation Commissions when an owner seeks to demolish a landmark. The former Italian Embassy was a free-standing urban mansion, in Washington, D.C. It consisted of a main building that housed the ambassador's residence, a chancery wing, and a courtyard. It was designed in Italian Renaissance Revival Style and was a primary and integral component of the boulevard of distinguished buildings in that part of the City. In 2001, Bruce Bradley purchased the property, and planned to convert it, by partially demolishing and adding new construction, into condominium residences. He sought the advice of an architectural design team, which advised that although the property was not in an historic district or designated as an historic landmark, it was "clearly eligible for designation," and that, "should anyone file a designation application, it would likely succeed." Before going forward with plans for redevelopment, the owner twice met with an officer at the City's Historic Review Board, who stated that the office had no present plans for designating the structure. The owner entered into an agreement with a local preservation group, in which certain changes were made to the design of the proposed renovation, and the owner agreeing to preserve some of the historic interior features of the property—the latter being matters beyond the protection of the local historic preservation law—in exchange for its agreement not to propose the embassy for designation.

After the owner had applied for pre-construction and construction permits, the Historic Preservation Office ("HPO"), being alerted to the filing by the building department, applied to designate the property an historic landmark.[26] The buildings department nevertheless issued some of the requested permits before the Historic Preservation Review Board ("HPRB") completed its review of the designation application, which ultimately resulted in designation of the property as an historic landmark. As a result, the HPRB determined the construction permits had been issued in error because the development that the owner proposed for the property was inconsistent with the purposes of the Act. The HPRB's landmark designation stated:

> The three-story hip-roofed main block contains the original ambassador's residence, with one-story flat-roofed wings enclosing three sides of an open-air courtyard at the rear. The fourth side of the court is formed

26 Historic Landmark and Historic Preservation Act of 1978, D.C. Code § 6-1101, *et seq.*

> by the side of the original chancery wing, originally a long two-story hip-roofed block with its short end facing onto Fuller Street. A circa 1930s addition extends the original chancery in a similar two-story configuration along Fuller Street, creating an L-Shaped footprint overall. The embassy is faced in limestone with a terra cotta tile roof and sculptural embellishment concentrated at window and door surrounds; the simpler chancery is stucco with limestone trim and tile roofs.

The designation had the effect of delaying and ultimately precluding the demolition of the structure. The owner challenged the ordinance and its operation, but in *Embassy Real Estate Holdings, LLC v. D.C. Mayor's Agent For Historic Preservation*,[27] the District of Columbia Court of Appeals rejected the challenge. The owner argued that the HPRB had no power to prevent the issuance of the permit as the property was not yet a landmark when the applications were filed. The court ruled that the owner's argument was foreclosed by the Act's definition of "historic landmark," to include a "building ... and its site ... for which an application for [historic landmark designation] is pending" with the HPRB.[28] The regulations further provide that upon the "official filing" of an application for landmark designation, "the application is considered a pending application, and if the property is a proposed historic landmark, it is protected by the Act."[29] This included properties for which permit applications have already been filed.[30] There were mechanisms that aimed to mitigate any potential unfairness from such interim protection by requiring that when construction permits are pending, the HPRB must both hold a hearing *and* come to a final decision within ninety days of the application for landmark designation.[31] To meet this goal, the regulations provide that the buildings department be notified "[i]mmediately" after an application is officially filed, and the owner of the property subject to an application for landmark designation is to be notified of the same "[w]ithin ten

27 944 A.2d 1036 (D.C. App. 2007).

28 D.C. Code § 6-1102 (6)(B).

29 10-C D.C. Mun. Reg. § 209.

30 *See* D.C. Code § 6-1102 (6)(B) (providing that the HPRB "will determine within 90 days of receipt of an application pursuant to §§ 6-1104 to 6-1108 [referring to permits for demolition, alteration, subdivision and new construction, whether to list such property as an historic landmark.])."

31 *See* 10-C D.C. Mun. Reg. § 209.5.

days of an official filing."[32] Upon being notified of the application for landmark designation, the property owner is to advise the HPO within five days if there are any permit applications pending before the buildings department, so as to trigger the HPRB's expedited consideration.[33] In this case, the HRPB followed the statutory procedures and acted within the prescribed time.

5G1. DEMOLITION CROSS-CHECKS

The injunction against alterations to historic structures only takes effect once the designation is formal. Under many ordinances, until that time, an owner is free to make changes and even preemptively demolish the structure. Some ordinances, like that in the District of Columbia, contain cross-check provisions, which essentially delay any application for a building permit to alter and/or demolish a potentially historic structure until the preservation commission has had a chance to review it for its historic merit.[34]

5G2. DEMOLITION BY NEGLECT

Demolition by neglect occurs when a property owner intentionally or strategically allows an historic property to deteriorate to a point of no-repair. In this way, an owner gets to demolish or remove the property without compliance with historic preservation regulations. While in most cases, there seems a deliberate plan to develop the property, it is the case that some owners simply lack the means or worldly presence to comply with the duty to maintain that

32 10-C D.C. Mun. Reg. §§ 209.1 & 209.2; § 209.3.

33 *See* 10-C D.C. Mun. Reg. § 209.6.

34 *See generally,* Julia Miller, *Protecting Potential Landmarks Through Demolition Review,* www.nthp.org/law.html. *See e.g.,* Alameda City Code § 13-21-7; Santa Monica Mun. Code § 9.04.10.16.010 (as amended by Ordinance No. 2131; Boulder [Colorado] Revised Code § 9-11-23, Monroe [Connecticut] Demolition Delay Ordinance, §237-1(c), *http://www.cttrust.org/index.cgi/1049*;
New Castle County [Delaware] Code § 6.3.020(B); Municipal Code of Chicago § 13-32-230(a)-(c) and § 2-76-215; Boston Zoning Code, 85-1-85-8; Town of Weston [Massachusetts] Bylaws, Art. XXVI; Montgomery County [Maryland] Code, Part II § 24A-10; Keene [New Hampshire] Code of Ordinances, Art. IV, §§ 18-331 through 18-335; San Antonio Unified Development Code. Art. 4, § 35-455(b)(2).

is found in most historic preservation ordinances.[35] Apart from clear guidance on what kinds of alterations are allowed on historic properties, ordinances do well to impose affirmative maintenance responsibilities, prescribe remedies and enforcement authority against violations. Many state enabling legislation confers specific legal authority to local governments to require affirmative maintenance provisions and those affirmative obligations have been upheld by the courts, such as those that follow here.

The Montgomery County, Maryland ordinance requires a public hearing when charges of demolition by neglect are raised. If a property owner has been requested to maintain his property but refuses to do so, the ordinance allows the director of the county's Department of Environmental Protection to arrange for necessary repairs and charge the expenses to the owner. The ordinance provides:

> Demolition by Neglect
>
> ... In the event the corrective action specified in the final notice is not instituted within the time allotted, the Director may institute, perform and complete the necessary remedial work to prevent deterioration by neglect and the expenses incurred by the Director for such work. Labor and materials shall be a lien against the property, and draw interest at the highest legal rate, the amount to be amortized over a period of 10 years subject to a public sale if there is a default in payment.[36]

The Portland, Maine ordinance permits its Department of Planning and Urban Development to order property owners to make necessary repairs to deteriorating buildings within specified time periods. The city also spells out in its ordinance procedures for appealing such orders. The ordinance provides:

---

35 *See Maher v. City of New Orleans,* 516 F.2d 1051 (5th Cir. 1975), *cert. denied,* 426 U.S. 905 (1976), in which a federal appeals court upheld an affirmative maintenance provision for the French Quarter in New Orleans, ruling that the provision was constitutional as long as it did not unduly burden the property owner; *see also Harris v. Parker,* Chancery No. 3070 (Cir. Ct. Isle of Wight County, Va. Apr. 15, 1985)(ordering repairs to be carried out in compliance with the affirmative maintenance requirements in the ordinance); *Buttnick v. City of Seattle,* 719 P.2d 93, 95 (Wash. 1986)(ruling that requiring an owner to replace a defective parapet on a historic building did not result in unreasonable economic hardship); *District of Columbia Preservation League v. Dep't of Consumer and Regulatory Affairs,* 646 A.2d 984 (D.C. App. 1994)(reversing approval of the demolition of a historic landmark in dilapidated condition caused by the owner's own actions).

36 Sec. 24A-9.

Preservation of Protected Structures.

(a) Minimum Maintenance Requirement.

All landmarks, and all contributing structures located in an historic district, shall be preserved against decay and deterioration by being kept free from the following structural defects by the owner and any other person or persons who may have legal custody and control thereof.

Deteriorated or inadequate foundation which jeopardizes its structural integrity;

Defective or deteriorated floor supports or any structural members of insufficient size to carry imposed loads with safety which jeopardize its structural integrity, members of walls, partitions or other vertical supports that split, lean, list or buckle due to defective material or deterioration which jeopardize its structural integrity;

Structural members of ceilings and roofs, or other horizontal structural members which sag, split or buckle due to defective materials or deterioration or are of insufficient size to carry imposed loads with safety which jeopardize its structural integrity;

Fireplaces or chimneys which list, bulge or settle due to defective material or deterioration or are of insufficient size or strength to carry imposed loads with safety which jeopardize its structural integrity;

Lack of weather protection which jeopardizes the structural integrity of the walls, roofs, or foundation.

(b) The owner or such other person shall repair such building, object, or structure within a specified period of receipt of a written order to correct defects or repairs to any structure as provided by subsection (a) above, so that such structure shall be preserved and protected in accordance with the purposes of this article....[37]

37 Section 14-690.

In addition to fines for "each day on which there is failure to perform a required act," in the case of willful or gross negligent failure, the ordinance makes the owner ineligible for a building permit for any alteration or construction on the historic landmark site for five years. And, for a period of 25 years, any alteration or construction on the property is subject to special design standards imposed in the ordinance, whether or not the property involved is historic.[38]

The Connecticut Trust has drafted a model demolition delay ordinance, which provides in part:

> Section 7. Regulatory Responsibilities: Historic and architectural review.
>
> (a) No person or entity may, without first applying and obtaining the approval of the commission, file an application for a demolition permit pursuant to section____ of the Municipal Code or for a building permit pursuant to section 9-15 of Municipal Code for
>
> (1) any demolition of any protected property or part thereof that is listed on, or under consideration for listing on, the National or State Register of Historic Places, or, in regard to the National Register, for which a National Register application has been approved for study by the State Historic Preservation Office,
>
> (2) any alteration of any such protected property or part thereof if that alteration is visible from a street other than a street which faces only the back of the building, or
>
> (3) any construction of a new structure in a historic district or on the site of a demolished protected property.
>
> (b) The commission shall adopt the Secretary of the Interior's Standards for the Treatment of Historic Properties (36 CFR Part 68), which shall serve as the guidelines for the Commission unless the Commission adopts design guidelines of its own.... The commission shall make reasonable

38 *Id.*

efforts to guide owners in preserving historic architectural character in a cost-effective manner.

(c) Any application for commission approval shall, at the latest, be placed on the agenda of the next commission meeting which occurs more than seven days after receipt of the application, except as otherwise provided in this subsection....

(d) Demolition of a protected property shall be approved by the commission only if the applicant establishes, to the satisfaction of the commission, that (1) there is no feasible nor prudent alternative to demolition or (2) the property, through no fault of any owner of the property after the effective date of this [chapter] ordinance, does not contribute to the architectural or historic character of the district and its demolition will not detract from the architectural or historic character of the district or area.

(e) This section shall not apply to any structure for which an emergency demolition or repair has been ordered by the municipality, but only if the emergency condition represents so immediate a hazard to public safety that demolition or repair cannot be deferred and the structure cannot be protected, secured, or stabilized by reasonable temporary measures until the commission is able to meet.

Section 7.1. Appeals Process.

* * *

(a) ...Any person aggrieved by a final regulatory decision of the commission may petition for a review of such decision to the board of preservation appeals within fifteen (15) days of the commission's decision. The board shall adopt rules and procedures for the aforesaid review of such decision within sixty (60) days of its appointment. Any decision by the board shall be based upon the same standards as are to be applied by the commission and shall include a statement of the reasons for the decision.

(b) Any person aggrieved by a decision of the board of preservation appeals, or by a decision of a municipal historic preservation commission if no board of preservation appeals has been created, may appeal to the superior court within fifteen days of the adverse ruling.

Section 8. Policy of municipal departments and agencies.

It shall be the policy of the municipality and its departments and agencies to give priority to the preservation of the municipality's historic architecture and character. All departments and agencies of the municipality, including but not limited to those dealing with planning, zoning, health, and safety, shall consider historic and architectural significance and preservation when making decisions concerning whether and how properties should be rehabilitated, mothballed, or demolished, including decisions concerning to whom dispositions of property will be made. Demolition shall be treated as an alternative of last resort and shall be utilized only when other reasonable alternatives do not exist.[39]

5H. INTERIOR LANDMARKS

THE POOL ROOM IN THE FOUR SEASONS RESTAURANT

39 Model Historic Preservation Ordinance, Conn. Gen. Stat. §7-148, as amended by Pub. Act. 13-181.

Although the Four Seasons Restaurant lost its lease inside a landmark building in New York City, while it resided there, it was an iconic and landmark public place in its own right. The struggle to conserve the restaurant gave rise to standards for designating all interior landmark spaces. These rules have stood the test of time and persist as legal standards.

The restaurant was notorious for its beauty and allure. It resided in the Seagram building, designed by Ludwig Mies van der Rohe. The interior of the restaurant was designed by the architect Philip Johnson. Both the building and the restaurant had been acclaimed as quintessential expressions of the International style. Inside, the ensemble of brass railings, metal draperies, a pool (the center of the Pool Room), and luxurious wall coverings evinced a "special historical and aesthetic interest" as required by the Landmarks Preservation Law.[40] In *Matter of Teachers Insurance and Annuity Association of America v. City of New York*,[41] the New York Court of Appeals upheld the application of a landmark designation of the interior of the Seagram Building. The court explained that the designation covered the architectural components, including things that might otherwise be viewed as movable personal property because of the ensemble.[42] What was also required for an interior landmark was that the building be open to the public. The owners argued that the court should distinguish between a restaurant and inherently public interiors such as railroad stations, lobbies and theaters, which are intrinsically dedicated to public use by their public assemblage purpose. Rejecting the assertion, the court stated that giving the ordinance its ordinary meaning, what is meant is that the space be usually, ordinarily and habitually open to the public, not that it be a place for public assemblage. An interior to which the general public is usually invited, regardless of its intended purpose falls within the ambit of the statute.[43]

40 The owners complained that the designation pertained as much to the character of the clientele as to the structure itself.

41 623 N.E.2d 526 (N.Y. 1993).

42 *Id.* at 531.

43 *Id.* at 529.

THE DEMISE OF THE FAMED RESTAURANT

In 2015, Aby J. Rosen, the owner of the Seagram Building proposed what he characterized as minor changes to the interior, including replacing the restaurant's carpet, removing the bronze and crackled-glass partition in the Grill Room between the bar and the dining area, and making operable the fixed upper panels of the walnut partition between the Pool Room's dining area and mezzanine private room. Initially, Rosen had proposed to remove the wine cellar between the two dining rooms turning them into bathrooms. While many speakers at the hearing suggested the changes would alter the aesthetic character of the space, Rosen's response was that "If something was designed in 1958 and it's not as functional in 2015, you ask for a change... I'm going to restore the Four Seasons back to its glory. I love the guys but their time has passed, and sometimes something great needs to go."[44] The Landmarks Preservation Commission approved the carpet replacement change, but not the others. Although the original space remained largely unchanged, after its lease expired and was not renewed, the restaurant itself moved to a new location a few blocks away in 2016. In July 2016, the furnishings from the restaurant were auctioned off in anticipation of the move.[45] Alas, after less than a year in the new space, the owners announced that it would close.[46] The old space is occupied by new restaurateurs.

5H1. SCOPE OF AN INTERIOR LANDMARK

The Philadelphia ordinance describes the "Public Interior Portion" of a building, eligible for landmarking as:

> An interior portion of a building or structure that is, or was designed to be, customarily open or accessible to the public, including by invitation. A public interior portion does not include an interior portion of a building or structure that was designed to be customarily open or accessible to the public, which interior portion has been significantly altered physically

44 Robin Pogrebin, *Landmarks Commission Rejects Plan to Change Interior of Four Seasons,* New York Times, May 19, 2015.

45 Curbed New York, Live: The Four Seasons Restaurant's Interiors are Being Auctioned Off Right Now, *https://ny.curbed.com/2016/7/26/12285540/four-seasons-restaurant-auction-live-updates.*

46 Florence Fabricant, *The Four Seasons Is Closing, Less Than a Year After Reopening,* New York Times June 7, 2019.

such that a substantial portion of the features reflecting design for public use no longer remain. Terminating use of an interior portion of a building or structure by the public shall not in and of itself constitute conversion of the design of such interior portion. A public interior portion does not include the interior portions of a building which was designed to be and still is used exclusively as one or more private residences.[47]

The interior may encompass those elements that are structural (columns, moldings) as well as things that are not, but which contribute to the ensemble of the interior (brass planters, chandeliers). Interior Landmarks are regulated just as exterior landmarks, that is, owners may not make changes to the character-defining attributes without permission from the regulating commission. What is not settled from the cases and ordinances is whether an owner can decide to convert the space from one allowing public access to private and whether the designation becomes void at that point.[48] The story of the Waldorf Astoria, formerly a hotel, but now predominantly private residences, is a good example of this dilemma. As a hotel, the Art Deco designed lobby was the kind of public space that provided the predicate for its landmarking. It was closed in 2016 for renovations. After conversion, that lobby area will be substantially smaller, and so will the landmark.[49]

51. HISTORIC DISTRICTS

An historic district is an area protected because it possesses a concentration of buildings, structures, objects or sites that are linked either historically or aesthetically—buildings constructed in the same distinct style or during a similar period in history. Famous historic districts include Seattle's Pike Place Market,

---

47 City Of Philadelphia Historic Preservation Ordinance, Ch. §14-203(252).

48 *See Saving America's Clocks, Inc. v. City of New York*, 33 N.Y. 3d 198 (2019)(upholding landmarks commission decision to allow renovations of interior space that would preclude public access, stating that "public access is a threshold condition, not an ongoing one," and "public access at designation is no more than the foothold that allows the Commission to exercise the police power to regulate private property.").

49 *City Landmarks Interior of Waldorf Astoria Ahead of Renovation, http://www.crainsnewyork.com/article/20170307/REAL_ESTATE/170309906/city-landmarks-interior-of-waldorfastoria-ahead-of-renovation-by-new-chinese-owners-anbang-insurance-group.*

New York City's Greenwich Village, Denver's LoDo District, Boston's Beacon Hill. There are more than two thousand historic districts in the United States.[50]

The Boulder, Colorado historic district ordinance provides for historic districts based upon a number of criteria:

> Historical Significance
>
> The district, as an entity, should show character, interest or value as part of the development, heritage, or cultural characteristics of the community, state, or nation; be the site of historic or prehistoric event(s) that had an effect upon society; or exemplify the cultural, political, economic, or social heritage of the community.
>
> 1. Association with Historical Persons or Events * * *
> 2. Distinction in the Development of the Community of Boulder * * *
> 3. Recognition by Authorities [such as] Historic Boulder, Inc., the Boulder Historical Society, local historians (Barker, Crossen, Frink, Gladden, Paddock, Schooland, etc.), F.L. Olmstead, or others in published form, as having historical interest or value.
> 4. Date of Construction* * *
>
> Architectural Significance
>
> The district should portray an environment in an era of history characterized by distinctive architectural period(s)/style(s); embody those distinguishing characteristics of an architectural type specimen, a good example of the common; include the work of an architect or master builder, known nationally, state-wide, or locally, and perhaps whose work has materials or craftsmanship which represent a significant innovation; or include a fine example of the uncommon.

50 For advice on creating historic districts, *see Ten Factors in Establishing Local Historic District Boundary Lines, https://savingplaces.org/stories/10-on-tuesday-10-factors-in-establishing-local-historic-district-boundary-lines/#.XA0XlPZFzRM.*

Architectural Identity ...display[ing] common characteristics or continuity, and represent a distinguished entity that possesses integrity of appearance, and/or feeling (mood).

1. Recognized Period(s)/Style(s): [such as] Victorian Revival styles, such as described by *Historic American Building Survey Criteria,* Gingerbread Age (Maass), 76 Boulder Homes (Barker), The History of Architectural Style (Marcus/Tiffin), Architecture in San Francisco (Gebhard et. al.), History of Architecture (Fletcher), Architecture/Colorado (Thorsen et al) and any other published source of universal or local analysis of "style".
2. Architect(s) or Builder(s) of Prominence:* * *
3. Artistic Merit: A skillful integration of design, detail, material, and color which is of excellent visual quality and/or demonstrates superior craftsmanship.
4. Example of the Uncommon: Elements of architectural design, detail, material, or craftsmanship that are representation of a significance innovation. [sic]
5. Indigenous Qualities: A style or material that is particularly associated with the Boulder area.* * *

Environmental Significance

The district should enhance the variety, interest, and sense of identity of the community by the protection of the unique natural and man-made environments.

1. Site Characteristics: The site should be of high quality in terms of planned or natural vegetation, and streetscape objects, i.e.: lighting, fences, sidewalks, etc.
2. Compatibility with Site: Consideration will be given to scale, massing, placement, or other qualities design with respect to its site.
3. Geographic Importance: As an entity it represents an established and familiar visual feature of the community,

having unique and irreplaceable assets to the city or neighborhood.[51]

Historic district regulations variously aim to preserve the "local vernacular" and the *tout ensemble.* The North Carolina Supreme Court, in *A.S.P. Associates v. Raleigh,*[52] observed:

> It is widely recognized that preservation of the historic aspects of a district requires more than simply the preservation of those buildings of historical and architectural significance within the district.... [Instead], just as important is the preservation and protection of the setting or scene in which [structures of architectural and historical significance] are situated. This "tout ensemble" doctrine, as it is now often termed, is an integral and reasonable part of effective historic district preservation.[53]

5J. URBAN PLANNING AND HISTORIC PRESERVATION

"Urban design [has become] shorthand for the composition of architectural form and open space in a community context,"[54] finding meaning and purposes from physical spaces, social equity and economic viability, toward the making of places of beauty, function and distinct identity.[55] Urban design is about constructing cities, guiding growth, and creating patterns of development to improve the quality of life. It starts with zoning ordinances, which are enacted based upon comprehensive plans and become law. Comprehensive plans are visioning documents that seek to assess the state of the community and to

51 *https://bouldercolorado.gov/historic-preservation/landmarked-buildings-and-historic-districts.*

52 258 S.E. 2d 444 (N.C. 1979).

53 *Id.* at 451.

54 Evyatar Erell, David Pearlmutter, and Terrence Williamson, Urban Micro Climate: Designing the Space Between Buildings 2 (2012).

55 *Id.*

project a future based on community values and demographics.[56] The rootedness of urban planning and design in the enacted law and the concomitant repertoire of strategies and tools mean that decisions on urban form will have long-term consequences.[57]

The morphology of urban planning and design cannot be reduced to a single metric, but consists of "art, social science, political theory, engineering, geography and economics," as great cities are defined by their qualitative characteristics—public spaces, diversity of population, and architectural styles.[58]

Land use ordinances are justified as the exercise of police powers and that predicate was broadly affirmed in *Village of Euclid v. Ambler Realty Co.*;[59] so long as the rationality of the relationship between the ordinance and its purposes is "fairly debatable," the court will defer to the legislative judgment.[60] In modern times, there are a plethora of other limits on private ownership serving similar ends. Among these are environmental laws[61] and affordable housing mandates.[62] Environmental laws aim to prevent harm to the natural world from acts that pollute the air, soil, and waters. In doing so, planned development must be analyzed for their impacts on the environment—how stream flow might be changed,

56 DANIEL MANDELKER, LAND USE LAW §3.13 (5th ed. 2012). Comprehensive plans typically contain current and future land use maps that establish land uses. Comprehensive plans and mapping serve to provide city leaders with mechanisms to carryout citywide decisions on the allocation of land uses, resisting pressures to make political deals and works to encourage rational development since information costs are reduced by *ex ante* decisions on what can be built as-of-right and where. *See generally* DAWN JOURDAN, ERIC J. STRAUSS, PLANNNING FOR WICKED PROBLEMS, A PLANNER'S GUIDE TO LAND USE LAW 3-4 (2014). Comprehensive plans are realized through zoning ordinances that regulate the intensity and location of uses pursuant to the vision laid out in the plans. Sometimes the consequences of the failure of development to conform with the comprehensive plan can be quite severe. *See e.g., Pinecrest Lakes, Inc. v. Shidel*, 795 So.2d 191 (Fla. Ct. App. 2001)(ordering the demolition of multi-family housing whose construction did not comport with comprehensive plan).

57 *Id.* at §3.16.

58 PETER CALTHORPE, URBANISM IN THE AGE OF CLIMATE CHANGE (2011).

59 272 U.S. 365 (1926).

60 *Id.* at 388.

61 Clear Water Act, 33 U.S.C §1251, Clean Air Act, 42 U.S.C. 7401, National Environmental Policy Act ("NEPA"), 42 U.S.C. 4321. *See generally* ANN POWERS, WETLANDS LAW AND POLICY; MILLER, POWERS, AND LONG, INTRODUCTION TO ENVIRONMENTAL LAW: CASES & MATERIALS ON WATER POLLUTION CONTROL (2008).

62 *See e.g., Alto Eldorado Partners v. Santa Fe*, 634 F.3d 1170 (10th Cir. 2011), *cert. denied*, 2011 U.S. Lexis 5378 (U.S. Oct. 3, 2011); *Cal. Bldg. Indus. Ass'n v. City of San Jose*, 351 P. 3d 974 (Cal. 2015).

how soil might be eroded.[63] Affordable housing mandates, by requiring developers to set aside units as affordable, sometimes in exchange for greater density of construction, aim to serve a basic human need.[64]

Historic preservation ordinances often exist as free-standing regulations, not integrated, but operating parallel to zoning and urban planning goals.[65] Sometimes, the ends of historic preservation, land use and environmental protection may be frustrated by changing visions of a desirable city plan. In cities, the imperatives to encourage and facilitate commerce stands out. Business improvement districts ("BIDs"), a form of public-private partnership operating within local governance, have been used in this way.[66] While the nomenclature varies—special improvement districts,[67] public improvement districts,[68] neighborhood improvement districts[69] are credited with helping to restore pride in the community by cleaning up and beautifying areas.[70] The positive effects of BIDs are undeniable—the provision of services paid for by the property owners, the betterment of the district, new investment, and the creation of distinct areas.[71] The net economic benefit from BIDs is also demonstrated, as most studies show

---

63 Under NEPA, agencies about to embark upon a major federal action must consider the impacts on the human and physical environment and that analysis must be contained in an environmental impact statement. 42 U.S.C. § 4332(C). NEPA is discussed in Chapter 7.

64 *Cal. Bldg Indus. Ass'n v. City of San Jose*, 351 P.3d 974, 980 (Cal. 2015) (affordable housing requirements do not constitute an exaction, only limits on use and finding valid legislative purpose in increasing affordable housing).

65 *See e.g., City of Tampa v. City National Bank of Fla.*, 974 So. 2d 408 (Fla. Ct. App. 2007)(architectural review commission lacked power to impose height limits not specified in zoning law).

66 Lorlene Hoyt and Devika Gopal-Agge, *The Business Improvement District Model: A Balanced Review of Contemporary Debates*, Geography Compass ¼ 946 (2007).

67 Hoyt and Gopal-Agge, *supra* note 66 at 946.

68 *Id.* (Texas).

69 *Id.* (Pennsylvania); *see also* Richard Briffault, *Our Localism: Part II-Localism and Legal Theory*, 90 Colum. L. Rev. 346 (1990). Briffault states "these variations make determining how many states authorize BIDs almost as difficult as calculating the number of BIDs. *Id.* at 417.

70 Briffault, *supra* note 69 at 448, *citing* David Henry, *As City Cuts Services, Firms Tax Themselves to Keep Streets Clean and Safe; It Works But Is It Good Policy*, N.Y. Newsday, Mar. 23, 1992, at 27 (community board chair who had opposed creation of New York City's 34th Street BID acknowledges, "It is no question that the streets are cleaner.").

71 *Id.* at 369, *citing* Heather MacDonald, BIDs Really Work, 6 The City J., Spring 1996, at 29. States and localities cite the successes of BIDs elsewhere in authorizing new BIDs. *See* Del. Code Ann. tit. 22, 1501(3) (1997); Business Improvements Districts Act of 1996, 1996 D.C. Law 134.

increases in property values and commercial activities.[72] But, the pursuit of improved business amenities, may sometime overshadow the values of historic properties in the vicinity. For instance, around the Grand Central Terminal in New York City is the new structure, One Vanderbilt, designed to have 77 floors, over 1,400 hundred feet tall, will loom over the historic terminal. The new structure was made possible by a recent rezoning of the area, the East Mid-Town Rezoning.[73]

5J1. OVERLAY ZONES

Perhaps the most efficient historic preservation strategy is an ordinance integrated with zoning regulations. One device is the overlay zone ("HPOZ"), an area of the city which is designated as containing structures, landscaping, natural features or sites having historic, architectural, cultural or aesthetic significance. It is a special zoning district placed over an existing zoning district, part of a district, or a combination of districts. The Flagstaff, Arizona Land Development Code states that overlay zones build on the underlying zoning, by establishing additional requirements and include requirements that are applied to property within the overlay zone *in addition to* the requirements of the underlying zoning district.[74] In case of a conflict between the requirements of the Landmarks Design Review Overlay District and the requirements of the underlying zoning district, the requirements of the former control.[75]

---

72 Hoyt and Gopal-Agge, *supra* note 66 at 956; Leah Brooks and Rachel Meltzer, *Does a Rising Tide Compensate for the Succession of the Successful? Illustrating the Effects of Business Improvement on Municipal Coffers*, in Municipal Revenues & Land Policies, Proceedings of the 2009 Land Policy Conference, at 275, 278. There are also identified negative societal effects, including the exclusion of the poor and street vendors from districts and greater distances between rich and poor areas, not unlike gated communities. By offering more services to neighborhoods willing to pay more in taxes, BIDs undermine the norm of equal provision of public services. *Kessler v. Grand Central Dist. Mgmt. Ass'n*, 158 F.3d 92, 124-25 (2d Cir. 1998)(Weinstein, J., dissenting). *See generally*, Richard Schragger, *Does Governance Matter? The Case of Business Improvement Districts and the Urban Resurgence*, 3 Drexel L. Rev. 49, 52, 54 (2010-2011)(questioning the claimed benefits of BIDs) .

73 Greater East Midtown Rezoning, *https://www1.nyc.gov/site/planning/plans/greater-east-midtown/greater-east-midtown.page.* Once One Vanderbilt is complete, the block-long stretch between 42nd and 43rd streets on Vanderbilt Avenue will become a car-free pedestrian plaza. There will also be a transit hall, open to the public, that connects the building and the streetscape to Grand Central below. Amy Plitt, *Midtown's soon-to-be supertall, One Vanderbilt, shows off its views The office tower is more than halfway toward its pinnacle,* Nov 2, 2018, *https://ny.curbed.com/2018/11/2/18052636/midtown-east-one-vanderbilt-skyscraper-construction.*

74 Ch. 10-15 Historic Preservation, City of Flagstaff Land Development Code.

75 *Id.* at 10-15-002-0003.

Los Angeles has developed an expansive program of HPOZs.[76] Adopted in 1979, there are now 35 designated HPOZs. They are established and administered by the Los Angeles City Planning Department (in concert with the City Council). Individual buildings in an HPOZ need not be of landmark quality on their own: it is the collection of a cohesive, unique, and intact collection of historic resources that qualifies a neighborhood for HPOZ status. HPOZ areas range in size from neighborhoods of approximately 50 parcels to more than 3,000 properties. Most types of alterations or improvements require written approval from the Planning Department. While most districts are primarily residential, many have a mix of single-family and multi-family housing, and some include commercial and industrial properties. Some of the advantages of HPOZs are increases in property value, and many homebuyers specifically seek out homes in unique historic neighborhoods and welcome the assurance that the qualities which attracted them to the neighborhood are more likely to endure over time. Also, there is the eligibility for property tax reductions. Under the Mills Act program,[77] owners of "contributing structures" (those structures that were built during the predominant period of development in the neighborhood and that have retained most of their historic architectural features) are eligible to enter into a contract with the City that can result in substantial property tax savings. The HPOZ Board, in addition to its formal role in the reviewing process, can often serve as an informal source of technical expertise and guidance on cost-effective ways to remodel properties to maintain and enhance their historic character, and may even suggest local contractors and crafts-persons who have worked on similar rehabilitation projects.

5J2. TRANSFERABLE DEVELOPMENT RIGHTS

Transferable development rights ("TDR") can be used to make up any economic losses that might result from an historic designation. A TDR allows landowners to sell development rights from their land to a developer or other interested party who then can use these rights to increase the density of development at another designated location. While the seller of development rights still owns the land and can continue using it, an easement is placed on the property that

76 *https://preservation.lacity.org/hpoz/homepage/about-hpoz-program.*

77 *http://www.ohp.parks.ca.gov/?page_id=21412.* The Mills Act is an economic incentive program for the restoration and preservation of qualified historic structures in the state, providing technical advice and tax state tax credits.

prevents further development. A TDR program protects land resources at the same time providing additional income to both the landowner and the holder of the development rights. Receiving districts can be located in places where urban growth or higher densities are desired or where urban services are available.[78]

5J3. PRESERVATION EASEMENTS

In exchange for a one-time federal tax deduction, owners voluntarily give up—in perpetuity—the right to make inappropriate alterations to their historic properties.[79] Historic landscapes and facades can be preserved permanently under conservation easements. Landowners retain many of their rights, including the right to own and use the land, sell it and pass it on to their heirs. The public benefits by the protected scenic views and preserved structures.[80]

5K. STATE ENVIRONMENTAL LAWS

THE OLD MONTEREY COUNTY JAIL

Monterey County Jail

78 *See e.g.*, Smart Growth America, Local Leaders Council, Transfer of Development Rights (TDR), Policy Primer, *https://www.smartgrowthamerica.org/app/legacy/documents/transfer-development-rights-policy-toolkit.pdf*; M. Walls and Virginia McConnell, Transfer of Development Rights in U.S. Communities, *www.rff.org/files/sharepoint/WorkImages/Download/Walls_McConnell_Sep_07_TDR_Report.pdf*; Jennifer Cohoon McStotts "A Preservationist's Guide to Urban Transferable Development Rights," National Trust for Historic Preservation, *https://forum.savingplaces.org/HigherLogic/System/DownloadDocumentFile.ashx?DocumentFileKey=bad2b890-b69a-721b-5b3b-86fcc48d6eeb.*

79 *See generally*, Anthony Robins, *The Case for Preservation Easements: When Municipal Ordinances Fail to Protect Historic Properties*, Thomas & Columbus, Inc., 2005, *https://anthonywrobins.com/wp-content/uploads/2013/01/WhenMunicipalOrdinances.pdf.*

80 *https://www.landtrustalliance.org/what-you-can-do/conserve-your-land/questions.*

The old county jail was built in 1931 in Gothic Revival style. The three-story structure was designed by Reed & Corlett, an architectural and engineering firm "responsible for numerous buildings in the San Francisco Bay Area from 1912 to 1933, many of which are still standing." The jail is located directly adjacent to the Monterey County courthouse in Salinas. It is approximately 40 feet tall, with some 19,000 square feet of floor space and consists of two primary wings, separated by a passageway. The original blueprints for the jail provided for a number of uses no longer consistent with modern penal practices ("a boys' department, vagrants' quarters, an insane cell, a padded cell, a delousing room, a darkroom, and a room for liquor storage"). Some of the jail cells "contain detailed and artistic graffiti done by prisoners."[81] In recent times, the jail housed César Chávez, the leader of the farm labor rights movement, for refusing to obey a court order to halt the United Farm Workers' lettuce boycott. His incarceration drew international attention, prompting visits from Coretta Scott King (the widow of Dr. Martin Luther King, Jr.) and Ethel Kennedy (the widow of Robert F. Kennedy) that galvanized the burgeoning farm workers movement. By the 1980's, the County had ceased using the structure as a jail. Since then, it has been used for records storage and as a temporary holding facility for prisoners appearing in court. In December 1999, by unanimous vote of its Board of Supervisors, the County directed its staff "to take necessary actions to provide for demolition of [the] old jail facility in Salinas." Various assessments of the jail preceded and followed the County's decision to demolish the structure. But, before the demolition could be undertaken, the project had to comply with the California Environmental Quality Act ("CEQA"),[82] which required certain determinations about the environmental impacts on historic properties. The City sought to proceed under CEQA by way of a "mitigated negative declaration," to avoid having to prepare an environmental impact report ("EIR"). The Architectural Heritage Association challenged that decision. In *Architectural Heritage Association v. County of Monterey*,[83] the California Court of Appeal, interpreted the CEQA in the context of historic preservation. The CEQA excuses the preparation of an EIR and allows the use of a negative declaration when an initial study shows that there is no substantial evidence that the project may

81 122 Cal.App.4th 1095 (Cal. App. 2004).

82 Pub. Res. Code § 21002.

83 122 Cal.App.4th 1095 (Cal. App. 2004).

have a significant effect on the environment.[84] If a straightforward negative declaration is not appropriate, the agency may permit use of a mitigated negative declaration (MND) "[i]f the initial study identifies potentially significant effects on the environment but revisions in the project plans 'would avoid the effects or mitigate the effects to a point where clearly no significant effect on the environment would occur.'"[85] If the project does not qualify for a negative declaration of either type, then a full EIR is required. The court ruled that the evidence did not establish grounds for either type of MND. To the contrary, there was substantial evidence in the administrative record supporting a "fair argument"[86] that the Old Jail was an historic resource (it had cultural significance from its association with an historic figure and the architecture, a combination of Art Deco, Gothic Revival and Classical was a fine exemplar of old Salinas and Monterey style); demolition would have a significant environmental impact (the building would be destroyed); and given the lack of evidence that the jail was in such poor condition, the proposed mitigation measures (photographic documentation, preparation of an historic monograph, salvage of certain architectural elements, and maintenance of a set of blueprints), were inadequate to reduce that impact to insignificance. An EIR was required before proceeding with a plan to demolish.[87] For a time, a remembrance of how we meted out justice and to whom, is preserved.

PRESERVATION OF THE OLD JAIL THROUGH RE-USE

Even though the old jail has since been enlisted on the National Register of Historic Places and was a finalist for consideration as part of a National Historic Park, efforts to demolish it continued.[88] The cost of rehabilitating it was estimated at nearly $30 million. Because the building was believed to be contaminated with asbestos and lead paint, the project would pose health risks to workers. A proposal to alter any historic part of the building would trigger an

84 Pub. Res. Code § 21064.5.

85 *Id.*

86 *But see Friends of Willow Glen Trestle v. City of San Jose,* 2 Cal. App. 5th 457 (Cal. App. 2016)("fair argument" standard of review does not apply to lead agency's decision that a resource is not a historical resource under Pub. Res. Code §21084.1).

87 122 Cal. App. 4th at 1119.

88 *https://www.youtube.com/watch?v=djVIVWFvAzk.*

EIR. In October 2017, the Monterey County Board of Supervisors, concluding that the building could and should be preserved, voted unanimously to begin a search for an appropriate adaptive re-use for the Old County Jail. A request for proposals ("RFP") was issued in December 2018, but received no responses, nor even any expressions of interest or clarifying questions, by the deadline. The board is now determined to preserve the building's façade even if the entire structure could not be saved. In March 2019, the board unanimously agreed to extend the RFP for another 60 days. The board also directed staff to conduct a more vigorous outreach effort to find potentially interested parties who could both submit a plan for the re-use and financial backing as required by the RFP.[89] As we discusss in Chapter 9, retooling structurally sound historic buildings serves the purposes of historic preservation while meeting other practical needs, like providing housing, offering an attractive space for an art gallery, a shop or accessible admininstrative offices.

5K1. STATE ENVIRONMENTAL LAW PROCEDURAL REQUIREMENTS

Many states have enacted environmental protection laws,[90] which have been construed to protect historic properties. In New York, the State Environmental Quality Review Act (SEQRA)[91] establishes a set of uniform regulations by which all state, county and local governmental agencies incorporate consideration of environmental impacts into their planning, review and decision-making processes. SEQRA requires that all governmental agencies determine whether the action they directly undertake, fund or approve may have a significant impact on the environment. In this respect, impacts to historic resources, such as buildings listed on the state or National Registers of Historic Places and archeological

89 Jim Johnson, *Old County Jail re-use gets another chance*, Monterey Herald (March 19, 2019).

90 To list a few: California (CEQA), Connecticut Environmental Policy Act (CEPA), District of Columbia Enviromental Policy Act of 1989 (DCEPA), Georgia Environmental Policy Act (GEPA), Hawaii Environmental Policy Act (HEPA), Indiana Environmental Policy Act (IEPA), Maryland Environmental Policy Act (MEPA), Massachusetts Environmental Policy Act (MEPA), North Carolina State Environmental Policy Act (SEPA), Puerto Rico Environmental Public Policy Act (EPPA), South Dakota Environmental Policy Act (SDEPA), Virginia Environmental Impact Report Procedure (VAEIR), Washington State Environmental Policy Act (SEPA), Wisconsin Environmental Policy Act (WEPA). For a comprehensive reference to state environmental policies and developments, *see https://ballotpedia.org/State_environmental_policy_acts.*

91 NY Envir. Conser. Law; 6 NYCRR Part 617.

sites, should be taken into account. If an action may have a significant adverse impact, agencies must prepare or request an environmental impact statement.

The California Environmental Quality Act,[92] declares that "it is the policy of the state that public agencies should not approve projects as proposed if there are feasible alternatives or feasible mitigation measures available which would substantially lessen the significant environmental effects of such projects."[93] A lead agency is responsible for determining whether an environmental impact report, a negative declaration, or a mitigated negative declaration is required for any project which is subject to the law.[94] The environmental impact report must assess the impacts to any historic properties in the path of development.[95]

Under the Environmental Rights Amendment of the state constitution, the citizens of Pennsylvania are guaranteed the communal right to clean air, pure water, and to the preservation of the natural, scenic, historic and aesthetic values of the environment.[96] The state's supreme court has interpreted the amendment broadly to prohibit unreasonable impairment of these rights.[97]

92 Pub. Res. Code § 21002.

93 *Id.*

94 Pub. Res. Code §21080.1.

95 Pub. Res. Code §21082.

96 Art I, Sec 27.

97 *See Pa. Envtl. Def. Found. v. Commonwealth*, 161 A.3d 911 (Pa. 2017)(broadly interpreting the scope of rights under the ERA; finding that all revenues received in exchange for use of public trust resources must be returned to the trust as part of the corpus; and declaring that under the first sentence of Art I, Sec 27, government may not "unreasonably impair" the right to clean air, pure water, and the like); *see also* Hayley Easton, *The Pennsylvania Environmental Rights Amendment: Implications for All Attorneys, The Courts' New View of the Environmental Rights Amendment, http://www.pbi.org/docs/default-source/default-document-library/easton.pdf?sfvrsn=0* (tracing the court's jurisprudence on the ERA).

CHAPTER 6:
RELIGIOUS PROPERTY

6A. HISTORIC RELIGIOUS PROPERTIES

THE COMMUNITY HOUSE AT ST. BARTHOLOMEW'S EPISCOPAL CHURCH

St. Bartholomew's Episcopal Church

The Community House was completed in 1928 by associates of architect Bertram G. Goodhue and complemented the adjacent Church building in scale, materials and decoration. The Church building was constructed in 1917 and is a notable example of a Venetian adaptation of the Byzantine style, built on a Latin cross plan. Significant features include its polychromatic stone exterior, soaring octagonal dome, and large rose window. Perhaps most significantly, Goodhue incorporated into his building the Romanesque porch of St. Bartholomew's former Church building. Designed by the renowned architectural firm of McKim, Mead & White, the porch is composed of a high arched central portal flanked by two lower arched doorways, all supported by slender columns. The doors themselves are richly decorated bronze, depicting Biblical themes. Together with the Church building, the Community House offered a variety of social and religious activities, including a sixty-student preschool, a large theater, athletic facilities (including a pool, gymnasium, squash court, and weight and locker rooms), as well as several meeting rooms and offices for fellowship and counseling programs. A community ministry program, which provided food, clothing, and shelter to indigent persons, was operated mainly from the Church building. Meals were prepared in a small pantry on the first floor and served in the mortuary chapel. Ten homeless persons were housed nightly in the narthex. The New York City Landmarks Preservation Commission designated both buildings as "landmarks." Over the course of three years, the church made three applications for a certificate of appropriateness to replace the Community House with an office tower; the first proposed a 59-story building and when that was denied, the Church proposed a 47-story building, which also was denied. The third application invoked the hardship exception under the Landmarks Law. At the public hearing held on the hardship application, the Church maintained that the building was inadequate to carry out the church's charitable purposes. The Commission denied the application and the Church sued the City, alleging among other things, that the Landmarks law was facially invalid and as applied to the Church; that it violated the free exercise clause and the establishment clause of the First Amendment by excessively burdening the practice of religion and entangling the government in religious affairs. The Church also claimed the application of the Landmarks law denied it due process because it applied different standards to charitable and commercial institutions. Finally, the Church maintained the landmarks law operated to take property without compensation.

In *Rectors, Wardens, & Members of the Vestry of St. Bartholomew's Church v. New York*,[1] the district court rejected the facial challenge to the landmarks law, as well as the establishment and entanglement claims, finding the law worked no more than an incidental burden on the practice of religion. The Second Circuit Court

1 728 F. Supp 958, 966-67 (S.D.N.Y. 1989).

of Appeals agreed with the trial court.[2] Even though the construction of the office tower might generate income and provide a better space for some of the Church's programs, enabling it to expand various ministerial and community activities, this was still not a violation of its First Amendment rights. The court noted *Employment Division v. Smith*,[3] in which the Supreme Court made clear that the free exercise clause prohibits "government regulation of religious beliefs *as such*,"[4] but does not constrain the government against restrictions on certain activities pursuant to its general regulatory powers, through valid and neutral laws of general applicability. The Landmarks Law was such a law. Unfortunately for the Church, because of their architectural designs, many religious structures were likely to fall within the neutral criteria of the regulation. The proper focus of the free exercise claim is on whether the church had been denied the ability to practice religion or coerced in the nature of those practices. The evidence failed to prove that the Church could not continue its religious practice in its existing facilities. On the takings claim, applying the *Penn Central* standard, the question was whether the Landmarks Law impaired the continued operation of the property in its originally expected use. The court found not—the Church could continue the existing character and religious activities in the current facilities; although the regulation may freeze the Church's property in the existing use and prevent the Church from expanding or altering its activities. In the end, the Church failed to show that the claimed cost of rehabilitation was justified by the condition of the building or that it could not find the funds—either through the use of its endowment or by borrowing—to meet those costs.

6A1. EXEMPTIONS FOR RELIGIOUS PROPERTIES

Religious structures may be the best exemplars of historic architectural styles. Churches and cathedrals stand tall. Their spires and buttresses reach to the heavens. The architecture is meant to create reverence for the spiritual and strive to connect with the divine. The ornate towers house bells used to summon the faithful to service. Church construction, although reflecting architectural styles of

2 914 F.2d 348 (2d Cir. 1990).

3 494 U.S. 872 (1990).

4 *Id.*

the time, was meant to endure for all time.[5] These characteristics make religious structures ready candidates for landmarking. Most preservation ordinances at the state and local level do not provide exemptions for religious property, but a few do, including ordinances in Chicago,[6] and Pittsburgh.[7] Some exemptions in the ordinances are narrowly tailored to apply only to places of worship, but not to property merely because it is owned by a religious institution, like schools or community centers. California allows religious property owners to exempt themselves from historic preservation if they can demonstrate a "substantial hardship ... likely to deprive the [institution] of economic return on its property, the reasonable use of its property, or the appropriate use of its property in the furtherance of its religious mission."[8]

Because religious institutions do not exist to earn a profit, applying the hardship exemption is necessarily different, depending on the whether the religious purpose is impeded by the application of the ordinance. If not, then any challenge to the historic preservation ordinance will likely fail.[9]

5 *See generally* Richard Kieckhefer, Theology in Stone (2004); Norbert Nussbaum, German Gothic Church (1994).

6 Mun. Code Of Chicago, Ill., ch. 2-120, § 660.

7 Code Of Ordinances, Pittsburgh, Pa. tit 11, ch. 1101.

8 Cal Govt Code §§ 25373(c), (d).

9 *But see First Covenant Church of Seattle v. City of Seattle,* 787 P.2d 1352 (Wash. 1990)(finding the Seattle landmark preservation ordinance and the designation of the church violated the church's First Amendment rights under the federal and state constitutions), *aff'd en banc* 840 P.2d 174 (Wash. 1992) (distinguishing *Smith*, finding the application of the liturgy exemption allowed the city to determine what is or is not religious purpose, and that the designation to the extent it limited the church's rights to dispose or alter church property imposed a substantial financial burden on the church).

6B. RELIGIOUS LAND USE AND INSTITUTIONALIZED PERSONS ACT

THE DECONSECRATED OUR LADY OF HOPE CHURCH

Exterior of Basilica of St. Louis

Interior of Basilica of St. Louis

The Church was built in 1925 in Italian Renaissance style. But, in the recent decades, the church had experienced declining numbers of clergy and parishioners. In 2004, the Roman Catholic Bishop of Springfield ("RCB") began a process of "pastoral planning," to assess the Diocese's financial and human resources on account of these demographic changes. The planning included the discontinuation of services at the church. Discontinuance would have required the removal of religious ornamentation and perhaps even destruction of the church to prevent their use for "profane" purposes. On news of the pastoral planning process, the historical commission created the single-parcel historical district, whose only building was the church. The RCB challenged the ordinance on the ground that it interfered with its free speech and religion rights and violated the Religious Land Use and Institutionalized Persons Act ("RLUIPA").[10] RUILPA prohibits a government from imposing or implementing a land use law that causes a substantial burden on religious exercise, unless in furtherance of a compelling governmental interest and is the least restrictive means toward that end. The RCB argued that the historic preservation law burdened its religious practice by intruding on its pastoral planning process, inhibiting future sale, the proceeds of which would benefit the parish, and by imposing continued costs of maintenance, insurance and security for the church. In *Roman Catholic Bishop Of Springfield v. City Of Springfield*,[11] the First Circuit Court of Appeals rejected a facial challenge to the local historic preservation law as a violation of the First Amendment and RLUIPA. While the ordinance was a "land use regulation" and the deconsecration process, a "religious exercise" within the meaning of RLUIPA,[12] the court explained that the mere enactment of the ordinance did not impose a substantial burden on the RCB. Whether a regulation amounts to a "substantial burden" would be determined by a number of factors, including whether the regulation appears to target a religion, religious practice, or members of a religious organization because of hostility to that religion itself; whether local regulators have subjected the religious organization to a process that may appear neutral on its face but in practice is designed to reach a predetermined outcome contrary to the group's requests; whether the land use restriction was "imposed on the religious institution arbitrarily, capriciously, or unlawfully, such as where, for instance, local regulators disregard objective criteria and instead act adversely to a religious organization based on the objections of a "small but influential" group in the community or where local regulators base their decisions on misunderstandings of legal principles. Essentially, the court explained, RLUIPA aims to prohibit an ordinance where the context raises an "inference" of hostility to a religious organization, even when the evidence does not necessarily show the explicit discrimination "on the basis of religion." No facts here showed such hostility. It did not single out or otherwise target religion, religious practice, or members of the RCB, nor was it imposed on the RCB arbitrarily, capriciously, or unlawfully. Even though the ordinance

10 42 U.S.C. § 2000cc *et. seq.*,

11 724 F.3d 78 (1st Cir. 2013).

12 42 U.S.C. § 2000cc-5(7)(A).

was not a neutral law of general applicability, because historic districts are specially created and pertain only to a particular property in limited areas, it did not single out for special benefit or burden RCB solely because of its religious beliefs. The ordinance did not target deconsecration as such, but merely required RCB to delay its decisions while the historical commission evaluated its application, a process that would ordinarily take no more than sixty days. The court found that the RCB failed to demonstrate any burden that caused it to modify its behavior.[13]

6B1. PUBLIC FUNDING TO PRESERVE HISTORIC RELIGIOUS BUILDINGS

While the First Amendment of the United States Constitution forbids discrimination based on religious preference, the language also proscribes the establishment of any religion. This injunction has not been read to deny historic religious structures the benefit of all government funds. Instead, they are treated as any other potential recipient, so long as the activities supported have a secular objective—like pre-schools and homeless shelters. This means that religious properties may be eligible for historic preservation grants.[14] However, some states have taken a different position. In *Freedom From Religion Foundation v. Morris County Board of Chosen Freeholders*,[15] the New Jersey Supreme Court ruled that public funds may not be used to restore and/or rehabilitate religious structures, even under the historic preservation programs. In that case, the grants purported to fund the preparation of construction documents and plans and the restoration of church buildings, towers, parish houses, windows, and other items, but all the churches had active congregations and all had conducted regular worship

13 *But see Chabad Lubavitch of Litchfield v. County, Inc. v. Litchfield*, 768 F.3d 183 (2d Cir. 2014)(RLUIPA applied requiring a determination whether a denial of a permit to alter historic property to a religious organization imposed a substantial burden upon the organization since the historic district commission applied subjective standards in conducting an individualized assessment of the proposed alterations; the historic preservation law was not a neutral law of general application, because of all the fluid criteria for designating a property for landmarking and for deciding whether to grant certificates of appropriateness for changes).

14 M. Edward Whelan, III, Acting Assistant Attorney General, Office of Legal counsel, *Authority Of The Department Of The Interior To Provide Historic Preservation Grants To Historic Religious Properties, https://www.justice.gov/olc/opinion/authority-department-interior-provide-historic-preservation-grants-historic-religious* (concluding that the Establishment Clause does not prevent the Department of the Interior from providing historic preservation grants to active houses of worship that satisfy the generally applicable criteria for funding under the Save America's Treasures Program).

15 181 A.3d 992 (N.J. 2018).

services in one or more of the structures for which grant funds have been or would be used. All twelve were Christian churches and several successful applicants stated that funds were needed to allow the church to offer religious services. This admission surely doomed their cause.[16]

16 On March 4, 2019, the Supreme Court denied a petition for certiorari in the case. 139 S. Ct. 909, 203 L. Ed. 2d 425 (2019).

Chapter 7:
Federal Property and Preservation Policies

7A. Archaeological and Natural Resources on Public Lands

The Grand Staircase Escalante

Grand Staircase Escalante

When the public owns lands on which archaeological or pre-historic sites exist, or other cultural heritage structures are located, a separate body of law governs. This is usually not the law of local governments. In the case of federal public lands, several statutes apply, including the NHPA. In the case of historic assets found on state lands, there are archaeological laws often dating from the 1920s, that have been supplemented by state environmental impact assessment statutes. For example, shipwreck under Lake George in New York include the Sunken Fleet of 1758 dating from the British and French & Indian War, and the military vessel "Land Tortoise." The New York State Navigation Law governs.[1] Under the federal Abandoned Shipwrecks Act of 1987, title for such vessels found in New York's Lake George vested in the State of New York.[2] Similar patterns of interwoven federal or state law can apply to state public lands, although the state laws primarily govern.

Dispute involving federal public lands, mostly in the western United States, are contentious, because of competing natural resources development demands on the sites. This is evident in the competing decisions under the Antiquities Act by Presidents Obama in 2016 and Trump in 2018 involving the designation of the Bear's Ears National Monument,[3] with sites rich in intangible cultural heritage of indigenous peoples, but also potentially rich in minerals that the federal government can sell or lease to private companies, benefiting the economy of the State of Utah.[4] Consider the earlier case of the Grand Staircase Escalante. In September 1996, President Clinton stood on the rim of the Grand Canyon in Arizona and signed a proclamation, pursuant to the Antiquities Act of 1906,[5] that created the Grand Staircase Escalante National Monument on 1.9 million acres in Utah. He did not first announce it to leaders in the state of Utah. In making the proclamation, the president protected what was left of the Escalante rivershed above Lake Powell – the canyon system that formed the western anchor of a legendary national park proposed in the 1930s. He acknowledged the scientific importance of the giant elevation gradient, with cliff barricade risers and plateau treads, called the "Grand Staircase." President Clinton's proclamation pointed to geologic and cultural treasures first observed by geologist and explorer John Wesley Powell. The area is remarkable for the colorful sandstone cliffs against deep canyons; picturesque rock facades; and prehistoric village sites. And, by the proclamation, there would be no mining in the area of the pristine Kaiparowits Plateau. President Clinton marked the boundaries of the monument large enough to serve as a laboratory for the study of a vast range of resources and migration patterns. But not everyone was happy with the proclamation. Some regarded it as in intrusion. The proclamation was challenged in

1 N.Y. Nav. L., art. 10.

2 43 U.S.C. § 2101, *et seq.*

3 Discussed below.

4 *https://www.washingtonpost.com/graphics/2019/national/bears-ears/?utm_term=.943e4ca2b23a.*

5 54 U.S.C. § 320301.

Utah Association of Counties v. Bush,[6] by the Mountain States Legal Foundation, which claimed that the Antiquities Act was unconstitutional because it violated the delegation doctrine; that only Congress has the authority to withdraw such lands from the federal trust; and that by creating the Grand Staircase Monument the President acted *ultra vires* and violated, among other things, the Property Clause of the Constitution[7] because the authority to manage federal lands rests exclusively with Congress. It also claimed that President Clinton's proclamation fell outside the limits of any statutory grant of power because it "failed to designate the requisite objects of historic or scientific value and did not limit the size of the monument to the 'smallest area' necessary to preserve the objects."[8] The court rejected the challenge on all counts. First, by the plain language of the Act, Congress has conferred upon the President the power to withdraw lands for purposes of conservation and there was adequate guidance given to the President in exercising that power. Where the act of the President is largely discretionary, a reviewing court is limited to determining whether the act was authorized, but a President's use of that discretion cannot be challenged. When President Clinton identified the geologic wonders of the area, among others, and determined that the area identified was necessary, he had fulfilled the requirements of the Act.

7A1. PRESERVATION UNDER THE ANTIQUITIES ACT: WITHDRAWAL AND REGULATION

By the Antiquities Act of 1906,[9] Congress expressed the national interest in preserving the natural wonders of the nation. The Act confers upon the president the broad power to declare by proclamation, that historic and prehistoric structures and other objects of historic or scientific interest situated on public lands be national monuments.[10] The Act reads:

> [T]he President of the United States is hereby authorized...to declare by public proclamation historic landmarks, historic and prehistoric structures, and other objects of historic or scientific interest that are situated

6 316 F. Supp. 2d 1172 (D. Utah 2004).

7 U.S. Const., Art. IV, § 3, cl. 2.

8 316 F. Supp. 2d at 1177.

9 54 U.S.C. § 320301.

10 *Id.*

> upon the lands owned or controlled by the Government of the United States to be national monuments, and may reserve as a part thereof parcels of land, the limits of which in all cases shall be confined to the smallest area compatible with proper care and management of the objects to be protected....[11]

Immediately after its enactment, President Theodore Roosevelt declared Devils Tower as the first monument and then three others in 1906, five more in 1907, and eight more in 1908 and 1909 before he left office. Perhaps his most important monument was the Grand Canyon, consisting of more than 800,000 acres. That proclamation was challenged and upheld in *Cameron v. United States.*[12] There, Ralph Henry Cameron, a mining claimant and Arizona politician began charging tourists a dollar to pass through his mining claims on the Bright Angel Trail which runs through the canyon. This practice interfered with the Santa Fe Railroad, which had a hotel on the south rim. The railroad asked the Department of Interior to investigate Cameron's mining claims. Even though the Department found Cameron's claims invalid, he refused to vacate. The federal government sued to evict him and Cameron defended his mining claims and further argued that the President lacked the authority to designate the Grand Canyon as a national monument. The Supreme Court unanimously disagreed, noting that the Grand Canyon was plainly an object of scientific interest as "*it is the greatest eroded canyon in the United States if not the world.*"[13]

Over the centuries, most presidents have proclaimed monuments of all nature and sizes—from the Harriet Tubman Underground Railroad in Maryland and Bears Ears National Monument in Utah, by President Barak Obama, to the African-American Burial Grounds in New York City and the Papahanaumokuakea Marine National Monument (covering 140,000 square miles) by President George W. Bush. President Obama's Bears Ears Proclamation stated:

> [f]or hundreds of generations, native peoples lived in the surrounding deep sandstone canyons, desert mesas, and meadow mountaintops,

11 *Id.*

12 252 U.S. 450 (1920).

13 *Id.* at 456.

which constitute one of the densest and most significant cultural landscapes in the United States.[14]

It goes on to describe the rich archeological character of the monument, revealing historic tools and implements for living that tell the story of ancient peoples. The area continues to serve the cultural and ritual needs of existing Tribes, including the Hopi, Zuni and Utes, among others. The area is unsurpassed in its natural beauty, diverse geology and vegetation—from cactuses to a wide palette of wildflowers, which in turn support innumerable wildlife species.[15]

The Antiquities Act gives the President the power to determine which federal agency is responsible for the management of a monument and most are managed by the National Park Service. In 1950, Congress amended the Act to prohibit further proclamations in Wyoming[16] and in 1980, the creation of monuments of more than 5,000 acres in Alaska, without Congressional approval.[17] Congress also has designated, expanded, and modified boundaries of, and approved funding for many national monuments.[18]

While most communities welcome proclamations (as they are a source of pride and tend to increase tourism), sometimes proclamations are resisted by the people of the state in which the monuments are situated, often because a proclamation withdraws the land from development and extractive operations. Despite that the Act only applies to federal lands, there was resentment to President Clinton's proclamation as it was seen as an imposition by the federal government; that proclamations should bow to the wishes of Utahns and their elected representatives. That resentment became even more pronounced with the proclamation of the Bears Ears National Monument by President Obama and his successor, President Trump responded. On December 4, 2017, he reduced the

14 *https://obamawhitehouse.archives.gov/the-press-office/2016/12/28/proclamation-establishement-bears-ears-national-monument.*

15 *Id.*

16 16 U.S.C. § 431(a).

17 16 U.S.C. § 3213(a).

18 *See generally,* David Harmon, Francis McManamon, & Dwight T. Pitcaithley, *The Antiquities Act: The First Hundred Years of a Landmark Law,* 23 Geo. Wright Forum 5 (2006); Carol Hardy Vincent and Kristina Alexander, *National Monuments and the Antiquities Act,* Congressional Research Service, July 20, 2010, www.crs.gov..

size of the monument by nearly 85 percent.[19] And, nearly twenty years after its proclamation, President Trump signed an executive order to draw new boundary lines for the Grand Staircase Escalante National Monument. The order introduced three new national monuments in this area named, west to east, Grand Staircase, Kaiparowits and Escalante Canyons.[20] The Antiquities Act grants the President the affirmative power to "reserve" lands, but specifically does not grant the power to modify or revoke such reservations.[21] And, nothing in the Act gives a successor president the power to reverse or alter a proclamation by his predecessor. President Trump's "reverse proclamations" have been challenged in several suits.[22]

7B. SURVEYING HISTORIC SITES

In 1935, Congress enacted the Historic Sites Act, which declared the national policy "to preserve for public use historic sites, buildings and objects of national significance for the inspiration and benefit of the people" and charged the Secretary of the Interior to restore, reconstruct, and maintain the same.[23] Perhaps the most important initial function of the Historic Sites Act was the dissemination of knowledge and information regarding historic resources.[24] Soon after, the Historic American Buildings Survey (HABS) was launched. Originally funded by the Works Progress Administration, HABS had an important role in

19 *https://www.whitehouse.gov/presidential-actions/presidential-proclamation-modifying-bears-ears-national-monument/.*

20 *https://www.whitehouse.gov/presidential-actions/presidential-proclamation-modifying-grand-staircase-escalante-national-monument.*

21 While the governor and other leaders of Utah praised the shrinking of the monuments, there was yet political fallout. Supporters of preservation reacted with great outcry and others responded with their pocketbooks. Companies such as Patagonia, cancelled conferences scheduled to take place in the state on account of the reverse proclamation.

22 *Wilderness Society, et. al., v. Trump,* Case No. 1:17-cv-02587 (D.D.C. Dec. 4, 2017); *Natural Resources Defense Council, et. al., v. Trump,* Case No. 1:17-cv-02606 (D.D.C. Dec. 12, 2017). For a further discussion of these issues, *See* Richard H. Seamon, *Dismantling Monuments* 70 Fla. L. Rev. 553 (2018); John Yoo and Todd Gaziano, *Presidential Authority to Revoke or Reduce National Monument Designations,* 35 Yale J on Reg. 617 (2018); John Murdock , *Monumental Power: Can Past Proclamations Under The Antiquities Act Be Trumped?*, 22 Tex. Rev. L. & Pol. 349 (2018).

23 54 U.S.C. §320101 [formerly 16 U.S.C. §462(a)-(k)].

24 See John H. Sprinkle, Jr., "An Orderly, Balanced and Comprehensive Panorama ... of American History": Filling Thematic Gaps within the National Park System, 27 George Wright Forum 269, 269-71 (2010) (discussing the motivations and impact of the HSA on survey efforts).

locating and documenting historic sites of national significance.[25] Architects and historians were put to work photographing and preparing measured drawings of important historic sites,[26] providing a base of knowledge about historic sites and their architectural forms.[27] The survey contains more than 30,000 measured drawings, 42,000 photographs and 15,000 pages of architectural and historical data for approximately 13,000 historic buildings from all fifty states, the District of Columbia, Puerto Rico and the Virgin Islands.[28]

As part of the first formal "listing" of historic properties, the HAS also commissioned the National Survey of Historic Sites and Buildings (the Historic Sites Survey), with the idea of evaluating important properties for inclusion within the National Park System. In some cases, the NPS would acquire historic sites and in other cases, would work to "restore, reconstruct, rehabilitate, preserve and maintain historic or prehistoric sites."[29] The NPS had the general authority to expend funds in support of preservation efforts on lands and buildings it owned and to make grants to non-federal owners of nationally significant properties.[30] Although broad, the NPS's acquisition authority was certainly not

25 *See* Lisa Pfueller Davidson & Martin J. Perschler, The Historic American Buildings Survey During the New Deal Era: Documenting "a Complete Resume of the Builders' Art", CRM, Fall 2003, at 49, 52-54.

26 *Id.*

27 In fact, the HABS records are the most widely used collection within the entire Library of Congress. *See* Heritage Documentation Programs, Nat'l Park Serv., *http://www.nps.gov/hdp/about.htm.* This work also continues to inform current preservation efforts. *See, e.g.*, Sally Zimmerman, A Documentary Legacy, Historic New Eng., Summer 2015, at 26, 26-29 (discussing the role HABS documentation plays in regional preservation efforts).

28 *Id.*

29 *See* 54 U.S.C. §320102(g); John Fowler, *Federal Historic Preservation Law: National Historic Preservation Act, Executive Order 11593, and Other Recent Developments in Federal Law*, 12 Wake Forest L. Rev. 31, 32-34 (1976). The "restore, reconstruct, rehabilitate, and preserve" standards laid out in the HSA were later adopted by the Secretary of the Interior as the appropriate preservation treatment approach, although not until 1992; *see also* A History of the Secretary of the Interior's Standards, Tech. Pres. Serv., Nat'l Park Serv., *http://www.nps.gov/tps/standards/history-of-standards.htm* (charting the evolution of the Secretary of the Interior's standards).

30 *See* Mary Ann King & Sally K. Fairfax, *Public Accountability and Conservation Easements: Learning from the Uniform Conservation Easement Act Debates*, 46 Nat. Resources J. 65, 81 (2006) (noting that "federal grants to states for preserving historic sites ... have a long provenance"); *but see* Gregory E. Andrews, Historic Preservation in the Private Sector, in The American Mosaic: Preserving a Nation's Heritage 208, 209 (Robert E. Stipe & Antoinette J. Lee eds., 1987) (explaining limitations on federal funding for preservation efforts).

unlimited,[31] as it had no authority to acquire property owned by a religious or educational institution, or property administered for the benefit of the public.[32]

Beginning in the 1950s, a new category of historic sites and buildings under the Historic Sites Act, to be known as Registered National Historic Landmarks, would recognize important properties not targeted for federal acquisition. Owners of properties of "exceptional value" would receive a certificate upon meeting certain programmatic conditions.[33]

7C. THE NATIONAL HISTORIC PRESERVATION ACT

THE MUCKLESHOOT TRAIL

Huckleberry Mountain

How should we preserve places where the physical evidence of a people's existence has been erased, but are still remembered by the people? Are these remembrances sufficiently valuable to society? The Muckleshoot Tribe is a federally recognized Indian Tribe, made up principally of descendants of tribes or bands

31 *See Historic Green Springs, Inc. v. Bergland*, 497 F. Supp. 839, 846 (E.D. Va. 1980) (noting that this acquisition authority is limited to properties of national significance).

32 54 U.S.C. § 320102(e).

33 A further discussion of the National Historic Landmark Program appears below.

that were parties to the Treaty of Point Elliott and the Treaty of Medicine Creek.[34] Ancestors to the present Muckleshoot Tribe included people from villages on the Green and White Rivers that form part of the drainage for Huckleberry Mountain in the Mt. Baker National Forest. For thousands of years, the ancestors used Huckleberry Mountain for cultural, religious, and resource purposes—uses that continue to the present day. This place of reverence would be lost by the proposed land exchange between the U.S. Forest Service and Weyerhaeuser, a giant timbering company. On March 28, 1997, Weyerhaeuser and the Forest Service executed an exchange agreement under which Weyerhaeuser conveyed to the United States 30,253 acres of land in and around Mt. Baker National Forest, in return for 4,362 acres of land in the Huckleberry Mountain area. The Forest Service land being exchanged consisted of old growth, commercial grade timber, that included portions of the Huckleberry Divide Trail, a site important to the Tribe and found to be eligible for listing on the National Register of Historic Places. The land Weyerhaeuser was exchanging was heavily logged and roaded. Weyerhaeuser intended to timber the newly acquired land.

The Tribe sued to enjoin the Huckleberry Mountain Exchange, alleging violations of the National Historic Preservation Act, seeking declaratory and injunctive relief. They alleged that the Forest Service did not fairly consider the impact of the exchange on the trail. In *Muckleshoot v. U.S. Forest Service,*[35] the Ninth Circuit Court of Appeals ruled that the Forest Service had failed to "take into account the effect of the undertaking on any district, site, building, structure, or object that is included in or eligible for inclusion in the National Register" and "afford the Advisory Council on Historic Preservation ... a reasonable opportunity to comment with regard to such undertaking," as required by Section 106 of the National Historic Preservation Act.[36] Because the area contained "properties of traditional religious and cultural importance to an Indian tribe, [TCPs]... determined to be eligible for inclusion in the National Register," the Forest Service was required to confer with the Tribal Historic Preservation Officer ("THPO"), regarding the identification of TCPs, and seek the approval of the Advisory Council on Historic Preservation before proceeding with the

34 The Tribe was organized pursuant to the Indian Reorganization Act of June 18, 1934, 25 US.C. §461-479.

35 177 F.3d 800 (9th Cir. 1999).

36 16 U.S.C. § 470f (9) (since recodified at 54 U.S.C. §306108). Although Section 106 is no longer in the recodified statute, for convenience, we continue to use it as a reference for the procedure.

undertaking.[37] In addition, the Forest Service was required to consider measures to mitigate any adverse effects on any TCPs. The Tribe provided information to the Forest Service to assist with the identification of historic sites, but the Forest Service did not earnestly evaluate the adverse effects—the loss of ancient paths and routes that enabled intercourse between peoples. Instead, it determined that maps using GPS technology and photographs of significant features along the trail that would be erased by the timbering, was enough. At the same time, it rejected, without good reason, other measures that would certainly have preserved the known cultural heritage, such as retaining easements or imposing covenants over the exchanged land.[38] The Forest Service failed to carry out its duties under the NHPA.

7C1. NATIONAL PRESERVATION POLICY

The enactment of the NHPA increased the role and prominence of the federal government in preserving historic properties, by including properties of local and state significance, along with those of national significance, within its ambit, authorizing grants to state and local governments, imposing procedural requirements upon federal agencies before impacting qualifying historic properties (Section 106), and creating a federal agency, the Advisory Council on Historic Preservation ("ACHP") to assist agencies with compliance.[39] The ACHP "makes recommendations on measures to coordinate activities of Federal, State, and local agencies and private institutions and individuals relating to historic

37 16 U.S.C. §470a(d)(6) (since recodified at 54 U.S.C. §302706).

38 177 F.3d at 809. The court went onto evaluate the Forest Service's fulfillment of its obligations under the National Environmental Policy Act ("NEPA"), 42 U.S.C. § 4331. With certain limited exceptions, in any major federal action, an agency is required to prepare an environmental impact statement that identifies and analyzes impacts on the environment. The EIS must fully analyze the cumulative effects of past, present and future projects. The court found the EIS to be inadequate, among other reasons, because it was one-sided (focusing only on the beneficial impact of the exchange and not also on the detrimental effects) and did not consider a range of appropriate alternatives. The court pointed out that while NEPA "does not mandate particular results," but "simply provides the necessary process" to ensure that federal agencies take a "hard look" at the environmental consequences of their actions, it is a burden nonetheless that must be borne. In this case, the Forest Service failed to take the necessary hard look at the environmental impacts of the exchange and similarly failed to consider adequate alternatives. NEPA is discussed in its own right below.

39 The scope of the National Historic Preservation Act, as a parallel set of duties to those of NEPA, is set forth in the landmark ruling of *WATCH v. Harris*, 605 F. 2d 310 (1979), discussed below.

preservation[.]"[40] It has promulgated extensive regulations governing Section 106 consultation.[41]

Most significant, the NHPA created the National Register of Historic Places, a comprehensive national survey of historic properties and districts, whether significant locally, at the state level, or nationally.[42] The eligible properties include districts, sites, buildings, structures, and objects that possess integrity of location, design, setting, materials, workmanship, feeling, and association; and

(a) that are associated with events that have made a significant contribution to the broad patterns of our history; or
(b) that are associated with the lives of persons significant in our past; or
(c) that embody the distinctive characteristics of a type, period, or method of construction, or that represent the work of a master, or that possesses high artistic values, or that represent a significant and distinguishable entity whose components may lack individual distinction; or
(d) that have yielded, or may be likely to yield, information important in prehistory or history.[43]

Nominations for listing are made through SHPOs and Tribal Historic Preservation Officers ("THPO") and final decisions on listing is done by the Keeper of the National Register.[44] Unlike local historic preservation ordinances, listing on the National Register does not constrain owners of properties in the use, alteration, or demolition of their property and while an owner can object to listing, a qualified property still remains eligible.[45] Listing or eligibility for the Register is honorific and serves as the basis for certain financial incentives, such as grants and tax credits, and gives the status for protection under the Section 106.

---

40 *Id.* § 304102(a)(1).

41 *See* 36 C.F.R. §§ 800 et seq. The regulations require the undertaking agency to consult with other parties regarding whether the project poses any identifiable adverse effects, *id.* at § 800.5, and to "seek ways to avoid, minimize or mitigate the adverse effects," *id.* at § 800.6(b)(1)(i).

42 *Id.*

43 36 C.F.R. § 60.4 (2016).

44 *https://www.nps.gov/subjects/nationalregister/how-to-list-a-property.htm.*

45 54 U.S.C. §302105; 36 C.F.R.§60.6(g).

Section 106 requires an agency undertaking a project expected to adversely affect a public or private site listed on the National Register of Historic Places to "take into account the effect of the undertaking on any historic property."[46] In fulfilling this requirement, the agency must consult with the respective SHPO or THPO and to seek input from the ACHP before proceeding with the undertaking.[47] Section 106 is purely a procedural provision and does not prescribe any particular treatment of an historic property, only consultation.

But the Section 106 (and environmental laws) procedures that "slow down" development are still met with consternation by would-be developers and miners. The recent listing of the Oak Flat campground is remarkable. The Oak Flat campground, about 100 miles north of Tucson, was added to the National Register of Historic Places, based in part on the site's spiritual ties to Western Apache tribes. The listing prompted outrage from Rep. Paul Gosar, R-Ariz., who insisted that it had no special significance to Native Americans and condemned the designation by the NPS as "bogus." The NPS deemed the "Chi'chil Bildagoteel" district, which includes Oak Flat, to be a "traditional cultural property," following a nomination from the U.S. Forest Service in consultation with the San Carlos Apache tribe. A proposed copper mine, using a mining method called "block-cave mining" would require the extraction of a huge amount of rock from underneath Oak Flat, eventually resulting in a 2-mile-wide crater as the surface collapses into the underground void, essentially destroying Oak Flat. But, by the listing of the site, mining cannot commence until the Section 106 and NEPA review processes have been completed. Rep. Gosar had repeatedly asked the NPS to withdraw the nomination and then backed legislation to privatize Oak Flat and surrounding lands, so that the mining could proceed without delay. Oak Flat is considered one of the sources of Ga'an, or Mountain Spirits, for the Apache people, the place of origin for the Apache group known as Dilzhe'e, from which many of today's Apache clans are descended. Even though the exact locations of holy places were not disclosed in the nomination report, keeping holy places secret was necessary to protect them from desecration. On the Yavapai-Apache reservation, Apache elders ask that members only speak of those sites in their own language. The Apache used the area not only for religious rites, but for collecting plants

46 54 U.S.C. § 306108.

47 54 U.S.C. §§306102(a)(5)(B), 306107, 302303, 306108; *see also* About the ACHP: General Information, Advisory Council on Historic Pres., *http://www.achp.gov/about.*

for traditional healing practices. Apart from Oak Flat's religious significance, it is an area rich with Apache archaeological resources that would be eligible for the National Register. The Forest Service and other archaeological surveys have unearthed evidence of the pre-historic Hohokam people and of 19th century Apache life, including villages and agricultural settlements, rock shelters and contrivances for processing agave.[48] The nomination forestalled mining for some time until the plan passed the procedural reviews and mining set to begin. The fight to prevent a "desecration" of sacred lands then moved to Congress. Several bills have been introduced to undo the land exchange that resulted in the mining company's ownership of the site.[49]

Apache Leap at Mining Project, Oak Flat, Arizona

In the case of National Historic Landmarks ("NHL"), the National Park Service must also be invited to participate in any consultation regarding a property so designated.[50] Under section 110(f), federal agencies must, to the maximum extent possible, undertake the planning and actions necessary to minimize harm to

48 Emily Bregel, *Historic designation of mining site provokes lawmakers' anger*, Arizona Daily Star, Mar. 14, 2016; *see also Oak Flat Listed on National Register of Historic Places*, Archeology Southwest, Archeology Today, *https://www.archaeologysouthwest.org/2016/03/20/oak-flat-listed-on-the-national-register-of-historic-places/; Oak Flat, Sacred Land Film Project, https://sacredland.org/oak-flat-united-states/* (November 26, 2018).

49 *See http://azminingreform.org/sites/default/files/docs/Save%20Oak%20Flat%20Act%20Grijalva%20 Press%20Release.pdf.*

50 *Id.*

any NHL.[51] While this section seems to impose higher duties upon agencies in the case of NHLs, the courts nevertheless have interpreted it as not imposing substantive protections.[52]

7C2. WHAT TRIGGERS SECTION 106 REVIEW

THE URBAN RENEWAL OF WATERBURY, CONNECTICUT

Urban renewal was urged on by the effects of the Great Depression, which caused society to see and evaluate the plight of the poor. The elimination of slums and redevelopment of central cities became prominent objectives. The goal of building new housing went hand in hand with slum clearance and in 1941, the Federal Housing Administration (FHA) adopted plans for slum clearance and urban redevelopment. The elimination of slums was thought to be a national policy, based on the belief that the externalities were contagions; that the transaction costs associated with the assembly and redevelopment of land in central cities by private enterprise was a large barrier to urban development; and that city governments had neither the legal nor the financial resources to undertake large-scale clearance and renewal efforts.[53] The original Act focused on clearance and redevelopment of a "predominantly residential" character.[54] Subsequent legislation embraced rehabilitation and conservation, carved out certain service projects that were not predominantly residential (such as

---

51 *See* About the ACHP, *supra* note 46. While Section 110(f) does not appear in the recodified NHPA, for convenience, it is used as a reference for the procedure.

52 *Presido Historical Ass'n v. Presidio*, 811 F.3d 1154 (9th Cir. 2016); *Nat'l Tr. for Historic Pres. v. Blanck*, 938 F. Supp. 908, 925 (D.D.C. 1996) (holding that federal agency was not required to expend additional funds to preserve historic resources, only to plan for their long-term preservation).

53 William J. Collins & Katharine L. Shester, Slum Clearance And Urban Renewal In The United States, Working Paper 17458, *http://www.nber.org/papers/w17458*, National Bureau Of Economic Research 4-7 (September 2011). "In 1949, Congress authorized the Housing and Home Finance Agency (HHFA) to assist locally planned urban renewal projects with grants of two-thirds (or in some cases three-fourths) of the net project cost to the city, where the net cost was defined as the difference between the total cost of acquiring and clearing properties and the income received from selling the cleared land." *Id.* at 4; *see also* Henry W. McGee, Jr. & Donald C. Bryant, Jr., *Gentrification and the Law: Combatting Urban Displacement*, 25 Wash. U. J. Urb. & Contemp. L. 43 (1983), *available at http://openscholarship.wustl.edu/cgi/viewcontent.cgi?article=1439&context=law_urbanlaw*, *citing* D. Mandelker, C. Daye, O. Hetzel, J. Kushner, H. McGee, & R. Washburn, Housing & Community Development 520 (1981); *see also* Chester W. Hartman, *Relocation: Illusory Promises and No Relief*, 57 Va. L. Rev. 745, 745 (1971) (offering similar assessments based on date from the National Commission on Urban Problems and National Association of Home Builders).

54 Collins & Shester, *supra* note 49, at 4-5.

hospital and university expansions), and encouraged citywide planning and code enforcement.[55] The most direct impact of an urban renewal project fell on the areas targeted for clearance, redevelopment, or rehabilitation. The theory was that by knocking down relatively low-quality housing and commercial buildings, the overall building quality would appear to improve.[56] Improving the physical condition of specific areas was believed to benefit the city "through a virtuous circle (e.g., less blight, less outmigration, and higher property values across the city), or at least by short-circuiting the process of deterioration."[57] Urban renewal attempted to make central-city locations more attractive to businesses as well as to residents; that firms and workers were willing to pay more to locate there for higher levels of "productive amenities," thus raising property values.[58] The pace of completion of projects was slow, usually taking years.[59] Though it began with fairly broad political support, urban renewal fell out of favor over the years and by 1974, the program had been abandoned, and the Housing and Community Development Act of 1974 enacted in its place.[60] The HCDA substituted block grants to cities, giving them wide discretion as to how to build communities, other than by slum clearance.[61] Before it was dismantled, urban renewal came to Waterbury, Connecticut.

55 A project typically began with "the creation of a Local Public Agency (LPA) that was 'enabled' under state legislation to undertake urban renewal activities and to exercise eminent domain powers. The LPA would identify an urban renewal area (typically characterized by 'blight' or signs of deterioration), hold public hearings, seek approval from the local government (e.g., city council), and then seek approval from the federal agency to proceed with specific project planning within that area. The project plans would include detailed information on current and proposed land use, changes in streets and utilities, aid for displaced residents and businesses, and estimates of the costs. Once approved, a combination of federal loans and grants would allow the project to proceed." *Id.* at 5.

56 *Id.* at 6.

57 *Id.*

58 *Id.* at 4-7. These amenities were found to have an "ambiguous effect on wages, however, because for any given rent level, workers are willing to accept lower wages to have access to the amenity, but firms are willing to pay higher wages." *Id.*

59 *Id.* at 5. "As of June 30, 1966, the last date on which detailed data are available, approved projects had cleared (or intended to clear) over 400,000 housing units, forcing the relocation of over 300,000 families, just over half of whom were nonwhite... For perspective, the 1950 Census of Housing characterized approximately 1.3 million units in metropolitan areas as 'dilapidated'... The proposed clearance areas included nearly 57,000 total acres (90 square miles), of which about 35 percent was proposed for residential redevelopment, 27 percent for streets and public rights-of-way, 15 percent for industrial use, 13 percent for commercial use, and 11 percent for public or 'semi-public' use." *Id.*

60 Housing and Community Development Act of 1974, 12 U.S.C. § 1706(e).

61 Mandelker, *supra* note 53.

The Water Companies, Waterbury, Connecticut

Waterbury, Connecticut was settled in 1674. Nicknamed the Brass City, it was once the center of the American Brass Industry. The brass industry in Waterbury began in the mid-18th century and provided livelihoods to people who could not make a living in the rocky, unproductive New England soil. The industry soared until World War II and beginning in the 1950s, the brass industry in Waterbury began a dramatic decline. The causes were several: the introduction of plastic, zinc, and aluminum, that replaced brass in household products; changes in industrial operations from local companies to large, national corporations with national networks, that made it difficult for the local companies to survive; and cheap overseas labor and new technologies that were better suited for modern factories. The number of brass workers dropped from its peak of 50,000 to 5,000 in the 1980's. It is a familiar tale for New England industrial towns—when industry leaves so does prosperity. Waterbury fell onto some rough times. In the early 1970s, a project to redevelop this declining city was adopted as part of the federal government's urban renewal programs. The project planned to demolish as many as 113 of the city's classic turn-of-the-century main street type buildings, despite evident historic merit. They were an eclectic collection of architectural styles, including Renaissance Revival, Richardsonian Romanesque, Greek Revival and Italianate. With funding from the Department of Housing and Urban Development ("HUD"), the local agencies set up demolishing these remarkable buildings. When the project was approved, the agencies determined that "there are no known significant historic, archaeological, or architectural sites or properties listed on, or being considered for nomination to, the National Register of Historic Places." In going forward, HUD concluded that there was no significant environmental impacts and that the processing of the Project could proceed. But HUD did not consult with the State Historic Preservation Officer (SHPO) about eligible properties before preparing the clearance, and there was disputed testimony that it also did not consult about listed or nominated properties. HUD did not prepare an environmental impact statement for the Project area and did not consult with the Advisory Council on Historic Preservation. No alternatives to demolition of buildings designated for demolition in the Project area were considered. Citizens who were concerned about the government's determination to erase all that was valued, along with all that was wrecked, formed Waterbury Action to Conserve Our Heritage ("WATCH"). They sued HUD and the local urban renewal agency to halt the razing of the beautiful buildings. They alleged that the defendants were heedless of their responsibilities under the National Historic Preservation Act (NHPA), Section 106 and under the National Environmental Policy Act, to evaluate the effects of the project. Prior to 1976, Section 106 of NHPA provided that

> The head of any Federal agency having direct or indirect jurisdiction over a proposed Federal or federally assisted undertaking in any State and the head of any Federal department or independent agency having authority to license any undertaking shall, prior to the approval of the expenditure of any Federal funds on the undertaking or prior to the issuance of any license, as the case may be, take into account the effect of the undertaking on any district, site, building, structure, or object that is included in the National Register. The head of any such Federal agency shall afford the Advisory Council on Historic Preservation established under sections 470i to 470n of this title a reasonable opportunity to comment with regard to such undertaking.

In 1976, Congress amended the NHPA to include protections also for properties eligible for inclusion on the National Register. That was the sticking point for WATCH, as the district court determined that the cut-off point for the application of section 106 was at the time when a grant and loan contract was executed. Because no properties in the project area were listed when the contract was signed in 1973, NHPA imposed no present duty on HUD to consider the effects of the project on eligible properties or properties listed after that time. This meant that even though at the time HUD actually funded the project, there were known historic properties, either listed or eligible in the path of the project, the agency was free to move forward without any constraints.

In the view of the Second Circuit Court of Appeals, in *Watch v. Harris*[62], this reading was too narrow and too literal. It reversed the district court, concluding that the provisions of NHPA do not cease to apply simply because an agency had preliminarily approved the project. Instead, they should apply until the agency had finally approved the expenditures of funds at each stage of the undertaking. To reach this conclusion, the Second Circuit found the language in the statute, "prior to the approval of the expenditures," must mean what the words purport and not "prior to the approval of the project," as the agencies urged. And, given that urban renewal projects are huge endeavors, "undertaking" must refer to the project's several phases. Even though the statute did not contain literal statements by Congress on this point, it could be inferred from the reasons and mechanics of the NHPA. Among other things, the statute created the Advisory Council on Historic Preservation to advise the President and to review plans for federal undertakings—to provide "meaningful review" of federally assisted projects which affect historic properties. The court found that because amended Section 106 required review as it pertains to both listed and eligible properties, a phase by phase interpretation ensured that the impact on many eligible properties will be considered once they are listed. In the end, the court inferred a congressional purpose, expanding over the years, to make certain that federal agencies give weight to the impact of their activities on historic preservation. Having this purpose in mind, surely Congress did not intend to adopt a strict cut-off date, at least as to grant and loan contracts, where the federal agency gives its final approval to the expenditures of federal funds only in stages. Indeed, the contract with the city explained that one of the purposes of phased approval was to ensure that the local agency does not take any step which, in HUD's opinion, might violate federal law, which surely included NHPA. Thus, Section 106, as amended, applied to require HUD and Advisory Council review as long as HUD retains the authority to make funding approvals pursuant to the grant and loan contract.

---

62 603 F. 2d 310 (2d Cir. 1979).

7D. NATIONAL HISTORIC LANDMARKS

THE PRESIDIO

The Presidio in San Francisco

The Presidio has been described as the birthplace of San Francisco and is noted for its diverse architectural styles and formal landscapes that illustrate the complex layering of construction over time. In the mid-twentieth century, the Presidio began a transition from a fully-functioning military base to the recreational preserve that it is today, starting with its designation as a National Historic Landmark District in 1962. In 1994, the National Park Service assumed control of the Presidio from the Army and managed the property under the Golden Gate National Recreation Area Act ("Golden Gate Act").[63] The Golden Gate Act sought to "preserve for public use and enjoyment certain areas of Marin and San Francisco Counties, California, possessing outstanding natural, historic, scenic, and recreational values, and ... to provide for the maintenance of needed recreational open space necessary to urban environment and planning."[64] The Act limited new construction within covered lands to "reconstruc[tion]," and specifically provided that "[a]ny ... structure which is demolished may be replaced with an improvement of similar size ...."[65]

---

63 16 U.S.C. § 460bb *et seq.*

64 *Id.* at § 460bb.

65 *Id.* at § 460bb-2(i).

The Main Post is sometimes referred to as the focal point of the Presidio and is managed by the Presidio Trust (the "Trust"), a wholly-owned government corporation created by the Presidio Trust Act.[66] Under the Presidio Trust Act, the Trust must fulfill the dual statutory purposes of preserving the historic and natural character of the Presidio and making the Presidio financially self-sustaining.[67] To meet those directives, the Trust in 2002 adopted the Presidio Trust Management Plan ('the plan"), which contemplated the extensive demolition and new construction on the Presidio's Main Post, including a new lodge, an expansion of the Presidio Theatre, an addition to the Presidio Chapel, and an archaeology lab. In the plan, the twelve small buildings of the lodge, which are aesthetically modeled after the historic Graham Street barracks, would be located to the Main Post area while also "strengthen[ing] the articulation of historic open spaces." This design aimed to ensure that the "scale, massing, height, and design" were "compatible with the surrounding historic environment."

Overall, the plan contemplated approximately 146,500 square feet of construction: 24,000 square feet of already completed construction plus 122,500 square feet of new construction. The new construction included 70,000 square feet for the lodge buildings, as well as additions to the Presidio Theatre, additions to the Presidio Chapel, the archaeology lab, and incidental new construction. In its final form, an Update slated approximately 148,010 square feet of buildings for demolition. Of those, 94,000 square feet are in the Main Post planning district,[68] then another 54,071 square feet of demolition in a nearby district.

After the Trust finalized the Update, the Presidio Historical Association and the Sierra Club (the "Associations") filed suit, challenging the Update on the grounds that the new lodge violated applicable statutes. In *Presidio Historical Ass'n v. Presidio*,[69] the Ninth Circuit Court of Appeals upheld the Trust's Update as falling within its authority under the Presidio act, then went on to consider whether the plan violated Section 110(f) of the NHPA. Because the Presidio is a National

66 Omnibus Parks and Public Lands Management Act of 1996, Pub. L. No. 104-333, 110 Stat. 4097 (codified at 16 U.S.C. § 460bb app.) ("Presidio Trust Act" or "PTA").

67 PTA §§ 101(5), (6), (7).

68 This number included 59,417 square feet under new demolition plans; 32,259 square feet of new demolition (Buildings 204, 231, and 230) attributable to a related project renovating Doyle Drive; and 2,263 square feet of already completed demolition.

69 811 F.3d 1154 (9th Cir. 2016).

Historic Landmark District, any project that alters the Presidio's structures is subject to section 110(f) of the NHPA.[70] Section 110(f) provides that "prior to the approval of any Federal undertaking that may directly and adversely affect any National Historic Landmark, the head of the responsible Federal agency shall to the maximum extent possible undertake such planning and actions as may be necessary to minimize harm to the landmark."[71] The court found that while the Trust had fulfilled its duty to consult (with state historical preservation officers, the ACHP and the public) it failed to comply with the additional requirements of Section 110(f) to "minimize harm to the landmark to the maximum extent possible."[72] Nonetheless, the court found that this directive merely contemplates procedural duties, a "higher standard for agency planning in relation to landmarks before the agency brings the matter to the council," but no substantive duties. This means that the agency should at least "consider prudent and feasible alternatives" to avoid adverse effects, which obligation stands on top of the more general duty in the Section 106 consultation process to "seek ways to avoid, minimize or mitigate ... adverse effects." The Trust needed to thoroughly consider—rather than simply identify and catalog—prudent and feasible alternatives to its proposed lodge design and in its planning process. The Trust met this heightened standard. Among other things, after hearing from the National Park Service, it changed the original proposal, reducing the footprint, scale, massing, and height of the proposed lodge; breaking up the mass into separate buildings ... or removing the lodge from the Main Post. It reduced the total square footage from its earlier proposals, and adopted at least a partially historically integrated design concept. The Trust also considered possible lodging alternatives, but rejected them as not feasible. The final plan was arrived at after extensive public engagement. Under the terms of Section 110(f), the Trust was not obligated to agree with the National Park Service's or the Presidio Historical Association's views—it only had to give them full and reasoned consideration, which it did. In

70 54 U.S.C. § 306101. Section 110 was added to the statute in 1980. Pub. L. No. 96-515, 94 Stat. 2987 (1980) (codified as amended at 54 U.S.C.A. § 306101 et seq.) Among other things, agencies must seek to use historic properties available to them before embarking on construction or acquisition, 54 U.S.C. § 306101(a)(2), and must develop a preservation program for federally-owned properties, id. at § 306102.

71 *Id.* at § 306107.

72 Section 110(f) goes on to say that the responsible agency "shall afford the [Advisory] Council a reasonable opportunity to comment with regard to the undertaking." 54 U.S.C. §306107. The Associations do not assert that this portion of Section 110(f) is substantive, and the Advisory Council's affirmation in the memorandum of agreement that the Trust had afforded it an "opportunity to comment on the Undertaking" is in any event sufficient to satisfy this obligation.

fact, the Trust "incorporate[d] the majority of the recommendations outlined in the [Park Service's] report," and offered reasoned explanations where it deviated from the Park Service's preferred result. The Trust's procedural undertakings surely met the heightened standard of care imposed by Section 110(f) to undertake "to the maximum extent possible ... such planning and actions as may be necessary to minimize harm to the landmark."[73]

7D1. ENHANCED PROTECTION FOR NATIONAL HISTORIC LANDMARKS

Presently, there are more than 2,500 NHLs nationally with at least one NHL found in every state, with a range of values, from Elvis's Graceland in Nashville, Tennessee to Thoreau's Walden Pond in Concord, Massachusetts to the John D. Rockefeller Estate, Kykuit in Pocantico Hills, N.Y. and the First Peoples Buffalo Jump in Ulm, Montana.[74]

In 1980, amendments to the NHPA provided for the independent legal recognition of national historic landmarks.[75] After that, Congress required the National Park Service to establish detailed criteria for designating NHLs in one or more of five general resource categories—historic buildings, districts, sites, structures, and objects, and for giving notice to interested parties regarding pending nominations.[76]

The criteria under which a property with exceptional value, can become an historic landmark are: (1) association with past historical events; (2) association with important people; (3) association with ideals that have shaped the nation; (4) outstanding architectural design or construction; (5) properties that

73 54 U.S.C.§ 306107. *See also National Trust for Historic Preservation v. Blanck*, 938 F.Supp. 908 (D.D.C. 1996)(Section 110(f) does not itself mandate the preservation of historic buildings).

74 See National Historic Landmarks Program, *https://www.nps.gov/orgs/1582/index.htm.*

75 *See* National Historic Preservation Act Amendments of 1980, Pub. L. No. 96-515, §201, 94 Stat. 2987, 2988 (codified as amended at 54 U.S.C. § 320101).

76 See National Register Bulletin, How to Apply for National Register, Criteria for Evaluation (1997), *https://www.nps.gov/nr/publications/bulletins/nrb15/.*

characterize a way of life; and (6) places that may yield information about the nation's past, such as archaeological sites.[77]

Structures that have achieved significance within the past fifty years are generally not eligible for designation unless they are of "exceptional importance" and relocated structures, reconstructed buildings, and religious properties, unless the resource's significance stems from its architecture or historical importance (a secular basis), are generally excluded.[78]

A property becomes a National Historic Landmark when designated by the Secretary of the Interior; being nominated by the property owner or advocate for the property[79] and often through thematic studies commissioned by the NPS.[80] NHL designation remains, as it has always been, largely honorific,[81] although there are some direct and indirect benefits that can come from listing—impact review in the case of federal undertakings under Section 110(f) and possible financial incentives for conservation.[82]

77 See 36 C.F.R. § 65.4(a). These criteria are more stringent than the National Register criteria for eligibility; the property must evince exceptional value or quality in illustrating or interpreting the heritage of the United States in history, architecture, archeology, engineering and culture and that possess a high degree of integrity of location, design, setting, materials, workmanship, feeling and association. *See* Id.

78 36 C.F.R. §65.4(b).

79 *See* National Historic Landmarks Program, *supra* note 73; *Historic Green Springs v. Bergland*, 497 F. Supp. 839 (E.D. Va. 1980). A property can be determined eligible for NHL designation if the owner does not consent to its formal listing. To date, only six properties have been determined eligible for NHL status, but have not been listed, owing to owner objections. *See* National Park Service, Determination of Eligibility, *https://www.nps.gov/subjects/nationalhistoriclandmarks/eligible.htm.*

80 See 36 C.F.R. § 65.5.

81 *See* Julia H. Miller, A Layperson's Guide to Historic Preservation Law: A Survey of Federal, State, and Local Laws Governing Historic Preservation 2 (2008).

82 National Historic Landmarks, *http://npshistory.com/brochures/nhl1.pdf.*

7E. THE NATIONAL ENVIRONMENTAL POLICY ACT

SANDY BUTTE IN THE OKANOGAN NATIONAL FOREST

Sandy Butte, like the Methow Valley it overlooked, was an unspoiled, sparsely populated area and pristine. In 1978, Methow Recreation, Inc. (MRI), applied to the U.S. Forest Service for a special use permit to develop and operate the "Early Winters Ski Resort" on Sandy Butte and an 1,165-acre parcel of land it had acquired adjacent to the National Forest. The proposed development would make use of approximately 3,900 acres of Sandy Butte and would stimulate extensive commercial and residential growth in the vicinity to accommodate both vacationers and staff. An Environmental Impact Statement ("EIS") purported to evaluate the potential impact of the development of a sixteen-lift ski area to accommodate 10,500 skiers at a time, on water resources, soil, wildlife, air quality, vegetation, and visual quality. The study also assessed the impacts on the population—land use, transportation in the valley, demographic shifts and economic markets for skiing and other summer and winter recreational activities in the valley, and the energy requirements. The study went on to evaluate off-site impacts that each alternative might have on community facilities, socioeconomic and other environmental conditions in the Upper Methow Valley. This analysis was not site-specific. The study outlined steps that might be taken to mitigate adverse effects, but stated that these were merely conceptual and would be made more specific as part of the design and implementation stages of the planning process. The study concluded that although construction, maintenance and operation of the ski area would not have a measurable effect on existing and future air quality, the off-site development of private land during the severe meteorological inversion period would be affected. Without efforts to mitigate, even under a no-action alternative, the increase in automobile, fireplace and wood stove use would reduce air quality below state standards. Air quality mitigation standards considered included the development of a management plan, regular weatherization of new buildings, limiting the number of wood stoves and fireplaces, adopting monitoring and enforcement measures, and procedures to control dust and comply with smoke management practices. The study recommended issuing the permit. Methow Valley Citizens Council and three other organizations opposed the permit and sued to reverse the issuance. The magistrate ruled that the study was adequate as a matter of law. In *Methow Valley*

Council v. Regional Forester,[83] the Ninth Circuit Court of Appeals reversed, finding among other things, that the Forest Service failed to include in the EIS "a detailed explanation of specific measures which would be employed to mitigate the adverse impacts of the proposed action.[84]

In *Robertson v. Methow Valley Citizens Council*,[85] the Supreme Court concluded that the Ninth Circuit required too much of the agency and reversed. The Court explained that while NEPA expresses a broad national commitment to protecting and promoting environmental quality,[86] in the end, all it requires is an identification and study of adverse environmental impacts from a major federal action. The sweeping policy goals of NEPA are realized through the procedures that require agencies to take a "'hard look' at environmental consequences," and that provide for broad dissemination of relevant environmental information. But, NEPA does not mandate particular results, it only prescribes the necessary process. If the adverse environmental effects of the proposed action are adequately identified and evaluated, the agency is not constrained by NEPA from deciding that other values outweigh the environmental costs, although other statutes may impose substantive environmental obligations on federal agencies. NEPA merely prohibits uninformed— rather than unwise— agency action.

Although nothing in NEPA requires steps to mitigate adverse environmental consequences, implicit in NEPA's demand that an agency prepare a detailed statement on "any adverse environmental effects which cannot be avoided should the proposal be implemented,"[87] is an understanding that the EIS will discuss the extent to which adverse effects can be avoided. The Court of Appeals' conclusion that the study's treatment of possible mitigation measures is inadequate as it failed to fully analyze and plan to mitigate off-site effects was entirely erroneous. Although NEPA and Council on Environmental Quality regulations require detailed analysis of both on-site and off-site mitigation measures, there is no basis for concluding that the Forest Service's own regulations must also be read in all cases to condition issuance of a special use permit on consideration

83 833 F.2d 810 (9th Cir. 1987).

84 833 F.2d at 819.

85 490 U.S. 332 (1989).

86 83 Stat. 852, 42 U.S.C. §4321.

87 42 U.S.C. §4332(C)(ii).

(and implementation) of off-site mitigation measures. The Forest Service regulations were promulgated under a broad grant of authority "to permit the use and occupancy of suitable areas of land within the national forests ... for the purpose of constructing or maintaining hotels, resorts, and any other structures or facilities necessary or desirable for recreation, public convenience, or safety,"[88] and were not based on the more direct congressional concern for environmental quality embodied in NEPA. As is clear from the text of the permit issued to MRI, the Forest Service decided to implement its mitigation regulations by imposing appropriate controls over MRI's actual development and operation during the term of the permit. NEPA does not require a fully developed plan detailing what steps *will* be taken to mitigate adverse environmental impacts and does not require a "worst case analysis," only that significant effects be studied.

7E1. REVIEW OF MAJOR FEDERAL ACTIONS AFFECTING THE ENVIRONMENT

Only a few years after the passage of the NHPA, the "growing public concern about the quality of our natural environment prompted Congress to enact the National Environmental Policy Act in 1969,[89] designed to curb the accelerating destruction of the country's natural resources.[90] The forces animating the enactment of the NEPA were similar to those behind the NHPA—rapid industrialization, urban renewal, the creation of the interstate highway program, the imperatives of the Army Corps of Engineers to dam rivers, and the increasing use of toxic pesticides and fertilizers in agricultural operations. Rachel Carson's pivotal book, SILENT SPRING, helped to raise the alarm about environmental degradation.

NEPA established a national policy for a broad national commitment to protecting and promoting environmental quality.[91] This national policy serves to guide the interpretation of NEPA's provisions. NEPA requires that agencies prepare a

---

88 16 U.S.C. § 497.

89 42 U. S. C. § 4321.

90 Before the passage of NEPA, the federal government's work to preserve the quality of the air, waters and land, came under the Rivers and Harbors Act of 1899, 33 U.S.C. §401 (imposing civil and criminal sanctions for discharging refuse into the waters and starting construction work affecting the waters without a permit by the Army Corps of Engineers, and the Federal Water Pollution Control Act of 1948, 33 U.S.C. §1251, enacted to address the increasing levels of domestic sewage and industrial wastewater.

91 42 U.S.C. § 4331.

"detailed statement" of the environmental impacts of any "major federal action significantly affecting the quality of the human environment," which is defined to include the "preserv[ation of] important historic, cultural, and natural aspects of our national heritage.[92] This "detailed statement" is known as an Environmental Impact Statement (EIS). Among other things, the act "directs that, to the fullest extent possible ... all agencies of the Federal Government shall—

* * *

> (C) include in every recommendation or report on proposals for legislation and other major Federal actions significantly affecting the quality of the human environment, a detailed statement by the responsible official on—
>
> (i) the environmental impact of the proposed action,
> (ii) any adverse environmental effects which cannot be avoided should the proposal be implemented,
> (iii) alternatives to the proposed action,
> (iv) the relationship between local short-term uses of man's environment and the maintenance and enhancement of long-term productivity, and
> (v) any irreversible and irretrievable commitments of resources which would be involved in the proposed action should it be implemented."[93]

Every agency in the executive branch of the federal government has a responsibility to implement NEPA and the Council on Environmental Quality (CEQ), within the office of the White House, has promulgated regulations for compliance with this mandate.[94]

Despite its lofty promises, perhaps the most significant shortcoming of NEPA, as with NHPA, is that it establishes only procedural requirements, and imposes no substantive duty upon actors to work to address environmental injury. And,

92 42 U.S.C. §4332(b)(4).

93 42 U.S.C. § 4332.

94 40 C.F.R. §§1500-1508.

despite finding that an undertaking does threaten the environment, as the Supreme Court in *Robertson v. Methow Valley Citizens Council* makes clear, the federal government can yet proceed, so long as the threats have been identified and studied in the EIS. Perhaps the salutary effect of adherence to this procedure, is that by exposing a project to public view, an agency might rethink going forward if the negative environmental effects are severe.

7E2. OVERLAP WITH SECTION 106

NEPA defines the environment to include historic properties.[95] Consequently a NEPA review and Section 106 might overlap in any given action. Section 106 is triggered in the case of a federal undertaking that poses an adverse impact on properties on or are eligible for listing on the National Register of Historic Places.[96] That same federal undertaking, for example, the construction of a federal office building, might be a major federal action, triggering NEPA.[97] The ACHP has developed protocols for coordinating the Section 106 process with the NEPA environmental review.[98] In this guidance, the ACHP urges early coordination[99] and advises in some cases that NEPA review can be substituted for the Section 106 procedure.

95 According to the NEPA regulations, in considering whether an action may "significantly affect the quality of the human environment," an agency must consider, among other things: "unique characteristics of the geographic area such as proximity to historic or cultural resources" (40 C.F.R. § 1508.27(b)(3)) and "the degree to which the action may adversely affect districts, sites, highways, structures, or objects listed in or eligible for listing in the National Register of Historic Places," 40 C.F.R. § 1508.27(b)(8). The NEPA regulations also require that: "to the fullest extent possible, agencies shall prepare draft environmental impact statements concurrently with and integrated with environmental impact analyses and related surveys and studies required by the National Historic Preservation Act." 40 C.F.R. §1502.25(a).

96 *See* 36 C.F.R. §800.16.

97 *See* 40 C.F.R. §1502.18.

98 Council on Environmental Quality and Advisory Council on Historic Preservation, A Handbook for Integrating NEPA and Section 106 (March 2013).

99 "Federal agencies are encouraged to coordinate compliance with Section 106 and the procedures in this part with any steps taken to meet the requirements of ... (NEPA). Agencies should consider their Section 106 responsibilities as early as possible in the NEPA process, and plan their public participation, analysis, and review in such a way that they can meet the purposes and requirements of both statutes in a timely and efficient manner." The determination of whether an action is a "major Federal action significantly affecting the quality of the human environment," and therefore requires preparation of an environmental impact statement (EIS) under NEPA, should include consideration of the undertaking's likely effects on historic properties. A finding of adverse effect on a historic property does not necessarily require an EIS under NEPA. 36 CFR §800.8(a)(1).

7F. THE NATIVE AMERICAN GRAVES PROTECTION AND REPATRIATION ACT

THE KENNEWICK MAN

The early protection for artifacts and rites of indigenous peoples came only tangentially, primarily through the Antiquities Act of 1906, which protected natural areas from exploitation or development. But, the protections there only extended to things of cultural heritage found on federal lands in the declared monument. Even with the passage of the Native American Graves Protection and Repatriation Act ("NAGPRA"),[100] a narrow reading of the scope of coverage leaves the cultural heritage of some peoples vulnerable to violations of cultural rites, if not to exploitation.

In July 1996, teenagers going to a boat race discovered a human skull and bones near the shore of the Columbia River just outside Kennewick, Washington. The remains were of a man who hunted and lived, or at least journeyed, in the Columbia Plateau an estimated 8340 to 9200 years earlier, a time predating all recorded history, a time before the oldest cities of our world had been founded, a time whose primitive culture remains largely unknowable by modern scholars. He is known popularly as "Kennewick Man," but known as "the Ancient One" to some American Indians who now inhabit regions in Washington, Idaho, and Oregon, roughly proximate to the site on the Columbia River where the bones were found. Scientists wanted to study the remains, as one of the most important American anthropological and archaeological discoveries of the late twentieth century, but the tribes wanted to bury an ancestor, in accordance with the tribes' religious and social traditions, without further testing. The Secretary of Interior's experts began to examine the remains in detail. They first thought the remains were those of an early European settler. Yet, comparing the physical characteristics of the remains—measurements of the skull, teeth, and bones—with corresponding measurements from other skeletons, they found that the remains revealed characteristics unlike those of a European settler, but also unlike those of any known present-day population, American Indian or otherwise. The Secretary's experts cautioned, however, that an apparent lack of physical resemblance between the Kennewick Man's remains and present-day

100 25 U.S.C. § 3001.

American Indians did not completely rule out the possibility that the remains might be biologically ancestral to modern American Indians. Moreover, despite apparent morphological differences, the Secretary's experts noted that Kennewick Man's physical attributes were generally consistent with the very small number of human remains from this period that had been found in North America. But the anthropologists then found a stone projectile point embedded in the skeleton's upper hip bone. The object's design, when viewed with x-rays and CT scans, resembled a style that was common before the documented arrival of Europeans in the region. Relying solely on the age of the remains and the fact that the remains were found within the United States, the Secretary pronounced Kennewick Man's remains "Native American" and decided to award the remains to a coalition of Tribal Claimants. The Army Corps of Engineers and the Secretary denied the scientists' request to study the remains. The scientists sued to stop the transfer and the district court ruled in their favor. The Secretary of the Interior and the intervenor-Indian tribes appealed. The Tribal Claimants based their demand on the Native American Graves Protection and Repatriation Act ("NAGPRA").[101] In *Bonnichsen v. United States*,[102] the Ninth Circuit ruled that NAGPRA vests "ownership or control" of newly discovered Native American human remains in the decedent's lineal descendants or, if lineal descendants cannot be ascertained, in a tribe "affiliated" with the remains.[103] The court explained that the first inquiry is whether human remains are Native American within the statute's meaning: if the remains *are not* Native American, then NAGPRA does not apply. However, if the remains *are* Native American, then NAGPRA applies, triggering the second inquiry of determining which persons or tribes are most closely affiliated with the remains. NAGPRA defines human remains as "Native American" if the remains are "of, or relating to, a tribe, people, or culture *that is* indigenous to the United States."[104] The Court read the text of the relevant statutory clause to refer to the present tense, that the human remains must bear some relationship to a *presently existing* tribe, people, or culture to be considered Native American. Unfortunately for the tribes, the court found that given the limited studies to date, it was almost impossible to establish *any* relationship between the remains and presently existing American

101 25 U.S.C. § 3001 *et seq.*

102 367 F. 3d 864 (9th Cir. 2004).

103 25 U.S.C. § 3002(a).

104 25 U.S.C. § 3001(9).

Indians. Instead, the court found that the only evidence offered by the Secretary of a possible cultural relationship between Kennewick Man and modern-day American Indians was their oral histories, but this evidence was deficient. In the court's view, oral accounts inevitably change in the context of transmission; they include myths that cannot be considered as factual histories, and the value of such accounts is limited by concerns of authenticity, reliability, and accuracy. The record as a whole did not show where historical fact ended and mythic tale began. Said the court, the "8340 to 9200 years between the life of Kennewick Man and the present is too long a time to bridge merely with evidence of oral traditions."

And so, Kennewick man was taken to laboratory for study. But in 2016, through DNA analysis, researchers determined that the remains were indeed Native American. During most of the time, the remains had resided at the Burke Museum, the Washington State Museum of Natural History and Culture. They were repatriated to the tribes who claimed him as their ancestor on February 17, 2017.

7F1. NATIVE AMERICAN CULTURAL RESOURCES

NAGPRA was enacted in 1990, and as the name suggests, aims to protect the rights of Indian tribes and Native Hawaiian organizations, and their lineal descendants, to cultural items, including human remains, funerary objects, sacred objects, and objects of cultural patrimony. NAGPRA has three primary goals. First, the statute increases protections for Native American graves located on federal and tribal lands by providing for Native American control over cultural items excavated from such lands. Second, the statute outlaws commercial trafficking in Native American cultural items. Third, the statute provides a comprehensive structure for the repatriation of Native American human remains and cultural objects that were in the possession or control of federal agencies or museums. NAGPRA requires all federal agencies and federally-funded museums, except the Smithsonian, to compile inventories of the Native American human remains and funerary objects within their possession or control, as well as summaries of all other cultural items and to make efforts to repatriate them to the relevant Native American Tribe.[105] The agencies and museums must

105 25 U.S.C. §3002.

notify all federally recognized Indian tribes about the status of their collections and engage in consultations with the tribes to establish cultural affiliation. The statutory notification process is intended to disclose enough information to allow culturally affiliated tribes to enter consultations and then make a claim.[106]

THE SACRED METEORITE

As *Bonnichsen* shows, there has been a persistent debate over who ought to control "culturally unidentifiable" Native American cultural items. One creative solution is illustrated in the case of competing claims by the American Museum of Natural History in New York City and the Clackamas. Thousands of years ago, a meteorite crashed into Earth's surface. The Clackamas believe that "Tomanowos" came to the valley as a representative of the Sky People and that a union occurred between the sky, Earth, and water when it rested in the ground and collected rainwater in its basins. According to the tradition of the Clackamas, Tomanowos had healed and empowered people in the Willamette Valley since the beginning of time. The rainwater served as a powerful purifying, cleansing, and healing source for the Clackamas and their neighbors. Tribal hunters, seeking power, dipped their arrowheads in the water collected in the Meteorite's crevices. These traditions and the spiritual link with Tomanowos continued to be preserved through the ceremonies and songs of the descendants of the Clackamas. The Museum had purchased the Willamette Meteorite in 1906 and since then the unique scientific specimen had been on almost continuous display at the Museum, viewed by millions of visitors from around the world. The meteorite was the centerpiece of the Cullman Hall of the Universe in the Museum's recently opened Rose Center of Earth and Space. The Tribes claimed it as part of their cultural heritage. In June 2000, the museum and the Confederated Tribes of the Grand Ronde Community of Oregon signed an agreement under which the tribes would be given access to the meteorite for religious, historical, and cultural purposes, including an annual ceremonial visit in the Museum, while allowing the museum to retain possession of it for scientific and educational purposes.[107]

---

106 *See* 25 U.S.C. § 3002(b) (defining unclaimed human remains and objects); 25 U.S.C. § 3006(a).

107 *http://www.amnh.org/exhibitions/permanent-exhibitions/rose-center-for-earth-and-space/dorothy-and-lewis-b.-cullman-hall-of-the-universe/willamette-meteori.*

7G. PROTECTING NATIVE AMERICAN CULTURAL HERITAGE THROUGH NHPA AND ENVIRONMENTAL REVIEW

THE DAKOTA ACCESS PIPELINE

Dakota Access Oil Pipeline

Dakota Access, LLC ("DA") requested a permit from the Army Corps of Engineers ("ACOE") under the Clean Water Act and the Rivers and Harbors Act to construct a pipeline to discharge dredged or fill material into navigable waters. The contested area was located on "original treaty land" containing Oceti Sakowin ancestral lands. Only a half-mile from the Standing Rock reservation, it transects the reservation's drinking water supply route. The oil pipeline was projected to aid in transporting approximately a half-billion gallons of crude oil through four different states *per day*. The tribe challenged the issuance of the permit, alleging a failure to consult as required by Section 106 of the NHPA. In *Standing Rock Sioux Tribe v. United States Army Corps of Eng'rs*,[108] the court rejected the challenge, finding that even before DA had sought a permit, the ACOE had reached out to Standing Rock and other tribes, sending them a copy of the cultural survey prepared by DA (indicating no cultural properties or no adverse impact on any, in the path of the planned route), inviting consultation from the beginning. The ACOE received no response from Standing Rock

108 205 F.Supp.3d 4 (D.D.C. 2016).

but did receive comments from other tribes, which it considered. The ACOE made further attempts to engage Standing Rock's leader, attempting to arrange meetings and seeking help identifying the location of cultural resources. Only after several months, did the Standing Rock leader respond, simply objecting to "any kind of pipeline construction through ancestral lands." In all, ACOE held four meetings, visited the sites and placed conditions on the pipeline permit.[109] The court also pointed out that while ACOE used the DA's cultural studies as a starting point, nothing in the NHPA or regulations required that the ACOE prepare them in any case.[110] The court defined the relevant undertaking as only that which affected lands under the federal government's jurisdiction and not the entire length of the pipeline.[111] Concluding that the ACOE's determination of no adverse effect on traditional cultural resources was supported by the facts, the court dismissed the complaint as to NHPA violations.

NATIONAL PROTESTS

After the Tribe sued to halt the construction, citizens' protests began. They arrested construction activities that had been scheduled to begin five days earlier. At first there were only 15 to 30 people protesting the construction of the Pipeline, but soon that number had increased to 100, then thousands, from all over the country. In North Dakota, the protests became violent. Some who had camped out near the construction area broke through a fence to access the site and were met by private security guards and guard dogs hired by the pipeline company. North Dakota Governor Jack Dalrymple activated the National Guard to assist local law enforcement that had been monitoring demonstrations. More than 500 National Guard members were on active duty and multiple buses and military vehicles had been deployed to transport protesters from the site.[112] Entertainment celebrities and the 2016 Green Party presidential candidate, Jill Stein, were among those arrested. At times over the course of several months of protests, law enforcement used tear gas and sprayed water at crowds of demonstrators even as the temperature dropped below freezing. On November 25, 2016,

109 205 F. Supp. 3d at 32.

110 *Id.* at 32.

111 *Id.* at 31.

112 Rebecca Hersher, *Key Moments in the Dakota Access Pipeline Fight, https://nationalpost.com/pmn/news-pmn/a-timeline-of-the-dakota-access-oil-pipeline.*

the U.S. Army Corps of Engineers ordered protesters to leave some encampments on federal land within two weeks and the governor followed up with an evacuation order for the area, citing "harsh weather," but the protesters stayed. Authorities began forcibly removing the last remaining holdouts in the main protest camps in advance of spring flooding season. The pipeline opponents took their protests to Washington, D.C., demonstrating outside the White House and President Donald Trump's Washington hotel. Some protesters moved beyond shouting to sabotage—coordinated physical attacks along the pipeline, using torches to burn holes through empty sections of the pipeline at above ground shut-off valve sites.[113]

In this contest, politics became front and center as shortly after his inauguration, President Donald Trump issued an executive order directing the ACOE to expedite the review and approval process for the unbuilt section of the pipeline. Even with this directive, the ACOE was still required to comply with law and that included the NEPA.[114] After the ACOE issued the permit, in June 2017, the district court largely rejected the Tribes' claims of violations of NEPA, finding the ACOE's assessment of impacts in the EIS was sufficient except as it pertained to native fishing and hunting rights and on the issue of environmental justice.[115]

Even though the protests failed to stop the pipeline, the decision by the government and DA to move forward was not without consequence, both positive—indigenous cultural rights were affirmed—and negative—the cost of policing the protests was large and President Trump refused the governor's request for a disaster declaration for federal reimbursement and it was soon discovered that the pipeline leaked—hundreds of gallons. If nothing more, the protests proved the vital role of citizen engagement for elevating the value of preservation alongside that of economic interests.

---

113 *A Timeline of the Dakota Access Oil Pipeline, https://nationalpost.com/pmn/news-pmn/a-timeline-of-the-dakota-access-oil-pipeline.*

114 42 U.S.C. §4321.

115 *Standing Rock Sioux Tribe v. United States Army Corps of Eng'rs*, 255 F. Supp. 3d 101 (D.D.C. 2017). On March 25, 2020, after evaluating expert comments that the pipeline suffered from serious flaws that could result in extensive environmental harm in the event of a spill, the court ordered the ACOE to prepare an EIS. *Standing Rock Sioux Tribe v. U.S. Army Corps of Engineers*, 16-1534 (D.D.C. March 25, 2020).

7H. ARCHEOLOGICAL RESOURCES

Recognizing that archaeological resources are an irreplaceable part of America's heritage and are endangered by the unauthorized excavation and black market trading in the contents of archeological sites, Congress passed the Archeological Resource Protection Act of 1979.[116] The Act and amendments aim "to secure, for the present and future benefit of the American people, the protection of archaeological resources and sites which are on public lands and Indian lands, and to foster increased cooperation and exchange of information between governmental authorities, the professional archaeological community, and private individuals."[117] The statute prescribes the requirements for permits to excavate or remove any archeological resource on Federal or Indian lands and sets out requirements for record-keeping and handling of archeological collections.[118]

ARPA also prohibits damage or defacement to archeological sites and the selling, purchasing, and other trafficking activities, whether within the United States or internationally. It brings within its coverage similar conduct in violation of a State or local law, ordinance, or regulation. The penalties are substantial—for a felony offense, first time offenders can be fined up to $20,000 and imprisoned for up to one year. Second time felony offenders can be fined up to $100,000 and imprisoned for up to 5 years. These criminal penalties were substantial increases from those set in the Antiquities Act of 1906 ($500 and 90 days imprisonment). In addition, ARPA grants Federal or Indian authorities the power to prosecute violators using civil fines, either in conjunction with or independent of any criminal prosecution. A court or civil authority may use forfeiture of vehicles and equipment used in the violation of the statute as another means of punishment against convicted violators.

The 1988 amendments[119] purported to lead to better management of archeological sites on public land, directing managers to hold information about the locations and nature of these resources confidential unless providing the information would further the purposes of the statute and not create a risk of harm

116 16 U.S.C. 470aa-470mm.

117 *Id.*

118 *See also* 36 C.F.R. §79 for implementing regulations.

119 16 U.S.C. §470ii.

for the resources. The amendments also authorized the Secretary of the Interior to cooperate with avocational and professional archeologists and organizations in exchanging information about archeological resources and improving the knowledge about the United States' archeological record. Federal land managers were directed to "establish a program to increase public awareness of the significance of the archaeological resources ... and the need to protect such resources" and to plan and schedule archeological surveys of the lands under their control.

7I. INTEGRATION OF FEDERAL, STATE, LOCAL AND NON-PROFIT EFFORTS

Is preservation best accomplished by the federal government, state government, municipalities, or private entities? Who should do what in preservation? Or, who can do preservation best? At the federal level, principally are the Departments of the Interior and the Agriculture. But historic preservation is not the sole charge of the administrative agencies of these departments (NPS and the Forest Service); they must also manage public lands and forests, preserving them, promoting public use of them. Within the agencies, there are competing views on what and how to preserve—traditional conservation goals versus new programs related to regional heritage tourism and recreation, all of which compete for internal resources.

7I1 PRESERVATION AND POLITICS

As evident from recent moves by the current administration—reducing the size of national monuments, pushing for mining in sacred areas—preservation can be frustrated by politics. One particularly worrisome movement is the pending series of proposed changes to the rules for listing on the National Register. If implemented, they will slow down nominations and even prevent listing at a landscape scale, at least as it pertains to those that involve both federal and other land ownership. One proposed change states that if federal property is included in a nomination proposed by a SHPO, the federal agency would have the discretion to put the nomination on hold and keep it from being considered for listing, apparently at all. Such power would enable bureaucrats loyal to the administration's cause to decide what gets listed, without regard to the merits of the nomination. Nominations supported by local governments or politically marginalized persons or groups (tribes, community groups, main street managers) could all be thwarted.[120]

712. COMPETING MOVEMENTS AND IMPERATIVES AT THE LOCAL LEVEL

Outside of the federal government, there are probably more than ten thousand national, state, and local government preservation and historical organizations and there are hundreds of non-profit entities,[121] many having a single focus, within cities working alongside, but sometimes in opposition to local governments. It is often said that land use, like politics, is local.[122] But, relegating preservation goals to the vagaries and fiscal imperatives of municipal governments or to the sometimes opposed and fragmented interests of local nonprofits can lead to competition for funding and membership and decisions that tend to impede the cause of preservation.

713. THE CASE OF THE STRAND BOOKSTORE

The Strand Bookstore, New York

120 Federal Register, Vol. 84, No. 41, Friday, March 1, 2019, Proposed Rules.

121 *See* non-exhaustive list of organizations and networks in the Appendix; *see also* Georgetown University Historic Preservation Resources, National, *https://repository.library.georgetown.edu/handle/10822/761776.*

122 But this may be changing as states have undertaken to intervene and pre-empt local land use decisions that have the effect of freezing out otherwise non-threatening land uses, such as affordable housing. *See* John Infranca, *The New State Zoning: Land Use Preemption Amid a Housing Crisis,* 60 B.C. L. Rev. 823 (2019); Anika Singh Lemar, *The Role of States in Liberalizing Land Use Regulation,* 97 N.C. L. Rev. 293 (2019).

The contest between multiple interests and preservation philosophies was recently played out in New York City concerning the iconic Strand Bookstore. The building that houses the fabled institution is an 11-story Renaissance Revival structure that dates back to 1902. The store's slogan was "18 miles of Books." The Landmarks Preservation Commission described the bookstore as being the center of literary life in lower Manhattan; an intellectually recognized bookstore and destination. On June 11, 2019, it voted to designate the building as a landmark. The Commission rejected an offer of a preservation easement on the property. There were many different sides taken in the contest. The owner vigorously opposed the designation, fearing the maintenance burden would be a death blow, particularly in an era of e-commerce booksellers, like Amazon, whose lower infrastructure costs enable them to price-out bricks and mortar stores. The Commission's representation of the availability of financial assistance, including grants to maintain the building was not reassuring. The irony in the matter is that the City had offered Amazon, $2 billion in incentives to open a headquarters in Queens, New York. Scores of loyal Strand customers and writers (such as Gary Shteyngart, Art Spiegelman, and Fran Lebowitz) supported the owner; the store had provided them an environment conducive to creativity and inspiration. The Greenwich Village Society for Historic Preservation criticized the commission's decision for not including a larger group of nearly 200 buildings in the neighborhood it believed was worthy of landmark designation; that the Commission was "cherry picking" among the buildings to placate preservationists at the same time allowing development. Just last year, the City rezoned a nearby site for a $250 million, 21-story tech training center. Another advocacy group, the New York Landmarks Conservancy, supported the designation, believing that it honors the building and that this designation would pave the way for preserving others in the community, especially in light of the tech hub.[123]

Preserving one historic building is to be celebrated, but what about the community in which it resides? Will it be lost amid a forest of new unremarkable towers? Who should evaluate the evidence of historic or architectural merit? Should we be concerned about the rise of the professional preservationists, that they will marginalize the lay activist preservationists whose passions drove the

123 Elizabeth Kim, *The Strand Bookstore Is Now A City Landmark, And The Owner Hates It*, Gothamist (June 11, 2019); Corey Kilgannon, *Declare the Strand Bookstore a City Landmark? No Thanks, the Strand Says*, New York Times (Dec. 3, 2018).

movement early on. Even though listing on the National Register and qualification for tax credit requires adherence to national standards, usually interpreted by professional preservationists, we should do well to bring in planners, ethnologists, folklorists, agricultural economists, geographers, neighbors, and just plain folk, into the class of policy and decisionmakers on protecting cultural heritage.

Chapter 8:
Preserving Parks and Landscapes

8a. The Transportation Act of 1966

OVERTON PARK

Overton Park

Until the 1960s, roadbuilding proceeded at a brisk pace, surpassing many other government programs in terms of spending and human power. More roads meant more jobs, more business, more convenience, an easier drive to work. But there were pernicious effects, the program pushed multi-lane highways through city neighborhoods, uprooting thousands of individuals and destroying entire communities. Sometimes the reason for these routes had to do with saving an extra five miles per hour of speed on a curve or to smooth the way for truck traffic, sometimes destroying much scenic beauty that stood in the way of the automobiles.[1] In 1966, these concerns prompted the enacted of the Transportation Act of 1966, in which Congress declared a national policy: " ...that special effort should be made to preserve the natural beauty of the countryside and public park and recreation lands, wildlife and waterfowl refuges and historic sites."[2] This was the same year that Congress adopted the NHPA. The case discussed below was the first case by the Supreme Court to explain what the law required.

Overton Park is located near the center of Memphis, Tennessee. The park contains a zoo, a nine-hole municipal golf course, an outdoor theater, nature trails, a bridle path, an art academy, picnic areas, and 170 acres of forest. Despite these marvelous features, the imperatives of highway construction weighed in on the city. The city proposed to construct a six-lane, high-speed, expressway, that would sever the zoo from the rest of the park. Although the roadway would be depressed below ground level except where it crossed a small creek, 26 acres of the park would be destroyed. The state paid the city $2,000,000 for the 26-acre right-of-way and $206,000 to the Memphis Park Commission to replace park facilities that would be destroyed by the highway. The highway would become a segment of Interstate Highway I-40, part of the National System of Interstate and Defense Highways. I-40 would provide Memphis with a major east-west expressway which would allow easier access to downtown Memphis from the residential areas on the eastern edge of the city. Although the route through the park was approved by the Bureau of Public Roads in 1956, and by the Federal Highway Administrator in 1966, the enactment of §4(f) of the Department of Transportation Act prevented distribution of federal funds for the section of the highway designated to go through Overton Park until the Secretary of Transportation determined whether the requirements of §4(f) had been met. Federal funding for the rest of the project was, however, available; and the state acquired a right-of-way on both sides of the park. In April 1968, the Secretary announced that he concurred in the judgment of local officials that I-40 should be built through the park. Final approval—of the route as well as the design—was not announced until November 1969, after Congress had reiterated in the Federal-Aid Highway Act that highway construction through public parks was to be restricted. Neither announcement approving the route and design of I-40 was accompanied by a statement of the Secretary's factual

1 Bruce Seely, *A Republic Bound Together,* Wilson Q. 19 (Winter 1993).

2 49 U.S.C. § 303.

findings. He did not indicate why he believed there were no feasible and prudent alternative routes or why design changes could not be made to reduce the harm to the park. In *Citizens to Preserve Overton Park v. Volpe,*[3] petitioners challenged the Secretary's action as invalid, as it lacked these formal findings; that the Secretary merely relied on the judgment of the Memphis City Council. The petitioners also asserted that there was a "feasible and prudent" alternative to route I-40 through Overton Park—to go either to the north or to the south. Petitioners also claimed that I-40 could be built under the park by using either of two possible tunneling methods, and that, at a minimum, by using advanced drainage techniques, the expressway could be depressed below ground level along the entire route through the park including the section that crossed the small creek. And they argued that if these alternative routes were not "feasible and prudent," the present plan did not include "all possible" methods for reducing harm to the park. While the Supreme Court accepted that formal findings by the Secretary were not required, nevertheless, it was necessary for the Secretary to make the required statutory determination. The Court explained:

> Congress clearly did not intend that cost and disruption of the community were to be ignored by the Secretary.... protection of parkland was to be given paramount importance. The few green havens that are public parks were not to be lost unless there were truly unusual factors present in a particular case or the cost or community disruption resulting from alternative routes reached extraordinary magnitudes. If the statutes are to have any meaning, the Secretary cannot approve the destruction of parkland unless he finds that alternative routes present unique problems.[4]

The Court remanded the case back to the lower court for a plenary review of the Secretary's decision to see if the Secretary acted within the scope of his authority and if the Secretary's action was justifiable under the applicable standard.[5]

3 401 U.S. 402 (1971).

4 *Id.* at 412-413.

5 *Id.* Other courts have applied the rigid test outlined by the Court and have required credible evidence that there is no prudent or feasible alternative to the path chosen for a particular roadway and planning to otherwise minimize any impact. *See e.g., Druid Hills Civic Ass'n, Inc. v. Federal Highway Admin.*, 772 F.2d 700 (11th Cir. 1985).

The plans for I-40 were later abandoned and the park survives. Overton Park is now a part of a comprehensive plan that also includes the Martin Luther King, Jr. Riverside Park and the Memphis Parkway System.[6] However, it was not until the mid-1960s that black citizens were given unrestricted access to the Park. Before that, they could enter only on Thursday afternoons to visit the Memphis Zoo and Aquarium. The only other park facilities available to blacks in the city for most of the 20th century were Church Park on Beale Street and Douglass Park, which was specially developed for their use in 1914.[7]

8A1. THE CONSTRUCTION OF THE NATIONAL HIGHWAY SYSTEM

The federal government's big public-works programs under the New Deal continued after the Great Depression had abated, aided in great measure by the country's entry into World War II. President Roosevelt had brilliantly linked the building of infrastructure (roads, bridges, trails in national parks) to abating the unemployment crisis. In 1944, the Federal-Aid Highway Act appropriated a huge increase in federal aid, $1.5 billion over three years, for an expanded system of primary, urban, and secondary roads. The bill also authorized but did not fund a new network of interstate roads between cities. Although President Harry S. Truman tried to restrain federal spending on large government projects to control inflation, the growing number of cars on the roads made the case for a new highway system. To meet the car drivers' needs, many states resorted to the old mechanism of toll financing, the Pennsylvania Turnpike was the first, built with New Deal aid in 1939-40. When this proved to be a financially feasible method for road building, several others followed and by October 1953, 762 miles of toll roads were open with 1,077 more miles under construction. By 1963, there were 3,557 miles. In 1954, a federal highway bill created the Dwight D. Eisenhower National System of Interstate and Defense Highways. It is a network of limited access highways that traverse the country. President Eisenhower first encountered the German Autobahn during World War II and concluded that interstate highways were vital components of national defense and commerce. Today, there are just under 50,000 miles of U.S. interstates, the

6 Overton Park Conservancy, *http://www.overtonpark.org/ history.*

7 John Linn Hopkins, *Overton Park: The Evolution Of A Public Space*, Memphis Park, City Of Memphis, Public Commission Construction Office, Prepared For Ritchie Smith Associates Overton Park Master Plan September 1, 1987.

longest system in the world. They serve almost every major city and many pass through urban centers.

The 1954 Act authorized $25 billion over 12 years, to be provided by highway-user taxes (gasoline taxes and excise taxes on tires) deposited in a highway trust fund. The federal government pays 90% of the cost of construction, with states picking up the remaining 10%, but have the responsibility for construction, operation and ownership.[8]

8A2. THE IMPACTS OF HIGHWAYS

At the enactment of the Transportation Act of 1996, the then Secretary of Transportation, Alan S. Boyd, expressed concern for the total environment: "...The time is no longer with us when we can move ahead in locating transportation facilities and in designing them without being concerned with and aware of the impact on the environment. We have progressed far enough in affluence and in technical ability to make such disregard largely unnecessary and certainly undesirable."[9]

Section 4(f) of the Department of Transportation Act of 1966, as amended,[10] and §18(a) of the Federal-Aid Highway Act of 1968[11] prohibit the Secretary of Transportation from authorizing the use of federal funds to finance the construction of highways through:

> a recreation area, or wildlife and waterfowl refuge of national, State, or local significance... or any land from an historic site of national, State, or local significance...unless (1) there is no feasible and prudent alternative to the use of such land, and (2) such program includes all possible

8 Bruce Seely, *A Republic Bound Together,* Wilson Q. 19 (Winter 1993).

9 Alan S. Boyd, Wetlands for Waterfowl Conservation, Hearings, 90th Congress, First Session, U.S. Senate, Commerce Committee, Subcommittee on Merchant Marine and Fisheries, August 16, 1967.

10 "It is hereby declared to be the national policy that special effort should be made to preserve the natural beauty of the countryside and public park and recreation lands, wildlife and waterfowl refuges, and historic sites." 49 U.S.C. § 303.

11 23 U.S.C. §138.

planning to minimize harm to such park, recreational area, wildlife and waterfowl refuge, or historic site resulting from such use.[12]

Unlike the NHPA, whose provisions are largely procedural, §4(f) contains mandatory, substantive provisions. As explained above, in the first case to test the meaning of the requirement that there be no "feasible and prudent alternative," *Citizens to Preserve Overton Park v. Volpe*,[13] the Supreme Court stressed the importance of preserving historic sites, that this end is paramount to transportation needs.[14]

8A3. THE §4(F) TRIGGER

The trigger for §4(f) is "use" of public land dedicated for parks, recreation, wildlife or waterfowl refuges, or historic sites. Use of a Section 4(f) property occurs when land is permanently incorporated into a transportation facility, there is a temporary occupancy of land that is adverse in terms of the statute's preservation purpose; or when there is a constructive use, i.e., a project's proximity impacts are so severe that the protected activities, features, or attributes of a property that qualify it as §4(f) property, are substantially impaired. This means that the value of the resource will be meaningfully reduced or lost, such as by increased noise to a noise-sensitive feature (a campground or outdoor amphitheater).

If the Federal Highway Administration ("FHWA") determines that the impact is *de minimis*, in the case of publicly-owned parks, recreation areas, and wildlife and waterfowl refuges, where the impact will not adversely affect the activities, features, or attributes of the property or in the case of historic sites, where no historic property is affected by the project, no analysis to determine whether avoidance alternatives are feasible and prudent, is required. A *de minimis* determination must be made with consultation with consulting parties and public involvement,[15] and be supported with sufficient information.[16]

12 23 U. S. C. §138; 49 U. S. C. §303(f).

13 401 U.S. 402 (1971).

14 *Id.* at 412-413.

15 36 C.F.R. Part 800.

16 23 C.F.R. §774.7(f).

An alternative is feasible if it can be constructed as a matter of sound engineering. Prudence assesses safety or operational problems and whether the alternative will meet the project's needs; weighs the severity of social, economic, environmental impacts, and considers extraordinary costs.[17] Avoidance alternatives include no action or build, relocation, alternative actions (e.g., different mode of transportation), alignment shifts, and design changes. If the analysis of avoidance alternatives determines that there are no feasible and prudent alternatives, then the FHWA may only approve the alternative that causes the least overall harm to the §4(f) property.[18] In determining least overall harm, the FHWA may consider factors such as the ability to mitigate adverse impacts; the relative severity of remaining harm after mitigation, and the relative significance of each §4(f) property. The agency should ask whether the project alternatives result in edge takes of a park or will they cut through the middle and how will activities, features, or attributes of the §4(f) property be affected by various alternatives and to what degree. If all of the alternatives are determined to cause "substantially equal" harm to §4(f) property, then the FHWA may choose any one.[19]

The FHWA has promulgated programmatic agreements to be used in standard, non-impactful environments, to streamline the review of the project.[20] To date, there are five programmatic evaluations that have been approved for use nationwide: Independent Walkway and Bikeways Construction Projects; Historic Bridges; Minor Involvements with Historic Sites; Minor Involvements with Parks, Recreation Areas and Waterfowl and Wildlife Refuges; and Net Benefits to a Section 4(f) Property.[21]

---

17 FHWA Environmental Review ToolKit, *www.environment.fhwa.dot.gov/4f/4fAtGlance.asp*; *see also* 23 CFR §774.17.

18 23 CFR §774.3(c).

19 *Id.*

20 *https://www.environment.fhwa.dot.gov/legislation/section4f.aspx.*

21 *Id.*

8B. BATTLEFIELDS

GETTYSBURG NATIONAL PARK

Gettysburg National Military Park is the preserved place of the momentous Civil War battle. The battle was the largest and most costly in human terms to occur on the continent. It lessened the Confederacy's ability to successfully wage war and contributed to the ultimate preservation of the United States. It is the place that inspired Lincoln's most oft-recited Gettysburg Address. The stated legislative purpose of the park is: "to preserve the topographical, natural, and cultural features that were significant to the outcome of the Battle of Gettysburg; to mark the lines of battle and to preserve the monuments and markers that commemorate the struggle; to provide opportunities for people to learn about the Battle of Gettysburg in the full social, political, and cultural context of the Civil War and American History; to preserve the objects, artifacts, and archives that document the battle, its aftermath, and commemoration."[22]

More than thirty years after the battle, in 1894, Congress appropriated funds for the park:

> For continuing the work of surveying, locating and preserving the lines of battle at Gettysburg, Pennsylvania, and for purchasing, opening, constructing and improving avenues along the portions occupied by the various commands of the armies of the Potomac and Northern Virginia on that field, and for fencing the same; and for the purchase, at private sale or by condemnation, of such parcels of land as the Secretary of War may deem necessary for the sites of tablets, and for the construction of the said avenues; for determining the leading tactical positions and properly marking the same with tablets of batteries, regiments, brigades, divisions, corps and other organizations with reference to the study and correct understanding of the battle, each tablet bearing a brief historical legend, compiled without praise and without censure; fifty thousand dollars, to be expended under the direction of the Secretary of War.[23]

22 National Park Service, *https://www.nps.gov/gett/learn/historyculture/index.htm.*

23 *United States v. Gettysburg Electric Railway Company,* 160 U.S. 668, 679-680 (1896).

The appropriation was challenged by the railway whose lands would be acquired to mark the grounds where battle was fought. It argued that preserving the battlefield was not a proper use for the exercise of eminent domain power. The Supreme Court upheld as a valid governmental purpose the expenditure of federal funds for the creation and protection of the Gettysburg Battlefield in *United States v. Gettysburg Electric Railway Company.*[24] The court stated that "[a]ny act of Congress which plainly and directly tends to enhance the respect and love of the citizen for the institutions of his country and to quicken and strengthen his motives to defend them, and which is germane to and intimately connected with and appropriate to the exercise of some one or all of the powers granted by Congress must be valid."[25] So the park was created.

8B1. ADMINISTRATION OF BATTLEFIELDS

Apart from protecting national areas under the Antiquities Act, the federal government has been directly involved in protecting another area of historic interest, i.e., battlefields,[26] beginning after the Civil War. While important sites at Gettysburg on the battlefield were preserved immediately after the 1863 battle, Congress formally established Gettysburg National Park in 1895. It comprises 5,989 acres and contains the Soldiers' National Cemetery. There are more than 1,700 monuments and cannons placed in the park by battle survivors to commemorate their comrades who served or fell in battle. More than one million artifacts, printed texts, historic photographs, and other archival documents are kept on the site.

8B2. NATIONAL PARKS

By the Act of March 1, 1872, Congress established Yellowstone National Park in the Territories of Montana and Wyoming "as a public park or pleasuring-ground for the benefit and enjoyment of the people" and placed it "under exclusive

24 160 U.S. 668 (1896).

25 *Id.* at 681.

26 *See* Ronald F. Lee, *The Origins and Evolution of the National Military Park Idea pt. IV* (1973), *http://www.nps.gov/parkhistory/online_books/history_military/nmpidea6.htm* (charting the late nineteenth century movement to protect Civil War battlefields). These efforts continue today and still involve federal support. *See, e.g.*, American Battlefield Protection Program, Catalog of Fin. Domestic Assistance, *https://www.cfda.gov/index?s=program&mode=form&tab=core&id=2b2df69d1c 976e11de-585d7a341019c7.*

control of the Secretary of the Interior." Congress went on to establish additional national parks and monuments, many out of the federal lands of the West and placed management of them with the Department of the Interior and other monuments and natural and historical sites under the War Department. It placed the Forest Service with the Department of Agriculture. President Woodrow Wilson changed this allocation when on August 25, 1916, he signed the Organic Act,[27] which created the National Park Service, a new federal bureau in the Department of the Interior, with the responsibility for protecting all national parks and monuments then under the control of Interior and those parks to be established. The Act declared the Department:

> shall promote and regulate the use of the Federal areas known as national parks, monuments and reservations...by such means and measures as conform to the fundamental purpose of the said parks, monuments and reservations, which purpose is to conserve the scenery and the natural and historic objects and the wildlife therein and to provide for the enjoyment of the same in such manner and by such means as will leave them unimpaired for the enjoyment of future generations.

By Executive Order in 1933, President Franklin Roosevelt transferred fifty-six national monuments and military sites from the Forest Service and the War Department to the National Park Service.[28] The National Park System of the United States now consists of more than 84 million acres in fifty states, the District of Columbia, American Samoa, Guam, Puerto Rico, Saipan, and the Virgin Islands. Additions to the National Park System are now generally made through acts of Congress. The Secretary of the Interior is usually asked by Congress for recommendations on proposed additions. The Secretary is counseled by the National Park System Advisory Board, composed of private citizens, which advises on possible additions to the System and on policies for its management. Today more than 20,000 National Park Service employees care for America's more than 400 national parks.[29]

---

27 16 U.S.C. §1.

28 National Park Service, *https://www.nps.gov/gett/learn/historyculture/index.htm.*

29 National Park Service, *Quick History of the National Park Service, https://www.nps.gov/articles/quick-nps-history.htm.*

Pictorial evidence is valuable for charting the evolution of a rural landscape and verifying its historic integrity. Comparative views of Ebey's Prairie, Washington, photographed about 1900 and in 1983, indicate little change in the division of land, agricultural land uses, and arrangement of the farmyard cluster. (Pacific Northwest Regional Office, National Park Service)

A "'landscape' is a dynamic, hybrid medium that links various human and non-human entities." It is an area made up of a distinct association of forms, both physical and cultural [30] The NHPA provides the basis for programs of the National Park Service for protecting historic landscapes. Since 1988, the NPS has developed programs for "cultural landscapes," which constitute "a type of cultural resource in the national park system in a management policy that mandated their recognition and protection. Preservation of cultural landscapes recognizes the importance of considering both built and natural features, dynamics of natural processes, and continued use."[31] Cultural landscape can refer to a variety of areas or constructs, from grand estates, farmlands, public gardens and parks, college campuses, and cemeteries, to scenic highways, industrial sites, city streets, and even works of art, narratives of cultures, and expressions of regional identity. The NPS defines "cultural landscape" "as a geographic area, including both cultural and natural resources and the wildlife or domestic animals therein, associated with a historic event, activity, or person, or that exhibit other cultural or aesthetic values." Four categories of cultural landscapes are recognized:

- designed landscape: a landscape that was consciously designed or laid out by a landscape architect, master gardener, architect

30 Carl Sauer, *The Morphology of Landscape*, 2.2 Geography 19–54 (1925).

31 Natiojnal Park Service, Mission, at *https://www.nps.gov/orgs/1557/pclp_mission.htm*

or horticulturist according to design principles or an amateur gardener working in a recognized style or tradition.

- vernacular landscape: a landscape that evolved through use by the people whose activities or occupancy shaped that landscape. Through social or cultural attitudes of an individual, family or a community, the landscape reflects the physical, biological, and cultural character of those everyday lives.
- historic site: a landscape significant for its association with a historic event, activity or person.
- ethnographic landscape: a landscape containing a variety of natural and cultural resources that the associated people define as heritage resources.[32]

The NPS provides activities for study and management of cultural landscapes and has set forth a standard for the stewardship of cultural landscapes. These include, significantly, working with adjacent properties where they are related to a protected cultural landscape. The policy considerations for these wider efforts at cooperation to conserve cultural landscape are as follows:[33]

- Adjacent lands significant to the physical, functional, or symbolic cultural landscape context of the NPS unit are identified.
- Direct impacts of adjacent land development on a park cultural landscape are identified, such as removal of woodlands; development and/or reforestation of traditionally "open" lands; alteration of historically significant field patterns; alteration of topography, streams, and watercourses impacting existing natural systems; and alteration of historic vistas.
- Indirect impacts of adjacent land development on a park cultural landscape are identified, such as increased commuter traffic on park roads, storm water runoff or restricted overland flow impacting park vegetation or generating erosion and pollution,

32 *Secretary of the Interior's Guidelines for the Treatment of Cultural Landscapes, https://www.nps.gov/tps/standards/four-treatments/landscape-guidelines/index.htm*; *see also,* National Park Service, Cultural Landscape Workshop: Landscapes and the National Register of Historic Places, ("Wyoming Workshop"), *http://wyoshpo.state.wy.us/pdf/LandscapesandtheNationalRegisterofHistoricPlaces.pdf.*

33 National Park Service, at *https://www.nps.gov/subjects/culturallandscapes/stewardship.htm.*

increased pressure for the park to serve local recreational needs, higher taxes or land values rendering local agriculture unprofitable, and use of pesticides and herbicides that may negatively impact natural resources.

- Potential impacts of adjacent land development on the cultural landscape context of parks are addressed through park involvement in the planning processes of local jurisdictions.

The National Park Service also treats a rural historic landscape as a separate category of property qualifying for listing in the National Register as a historic site or district. It is defined as:

> a geographical area that historically has been used by people, or shaped or modified by human activity, occupancy, or intervention, and that possesses a significant concentration, linkage, or continuity of areas of land use, vegetation, buildings and structures, roads and waterways, and natural features. ...[They] commonly reflect the day-to-day occupational activities of people engaged in traditional work such as mining, fishing, and various types of agriculture. Often, they have developed and evolved in response to both the forces of nature and the pragmatic need to make a living. Landscapes small in size and having no buildings or structures, such as an experimental orchard, are classified as sites. Most, however, being extensive in acreage and containing a number of buildings, sites, and structures—such as a ranch or farming community—are classified as historic districts. ...Distinct from designed landscapes, rural landscapes usually are not the work of a professional designer and have not been developed according to academic or professional design standards, theories, or philosophies of landscape architecture.[34]

Rural cultural landscapes, such as Ebey's Prairie, seen above, keep the romantic isolation of the prairie,[35] while designed landscapes like Riverside, Illinois

34 *See Guidelines for Evaluating and Documenting Rural Historic Landscapes, https://www.nps.gov/nr/publications/bulletins/nrb30/.*

35 *Id.*

(designed by Frederick Law Olmsted) reveal a vision for creating and connecting community in an otherwise desolate place.[36]

Local historic preservation ordinances specifically include "landscapes" as protected property. For example, the City of Eureka, California defines cultural landscape "as a geographic area that (1) has been used, shaped, or modified by human activity, occupation, intervention; or (2) possesses significant value in the belief system of a culture or society," and includes protections for designed and rural landscapes.[37] Cultural landscapes tell "the story of how places are planned, designed, built, inhabited, appropriated, celebrated, despoiled, and discarded"; the story of "the ditchdiggers and piledrivers, the streetcar workers and the railroad mechanics, the canal drivers and crane operators who represent class, ethnic, and gender history shaping the landscape in ways that have barely been studied."[38]

---

36 Wyoming Workshop, *supra* note 32, at 23.

37 *See e.g.*, Eureka, California, Code of Ordinances, Title XV, Land Usage, Ch. 157, Historic Preservation; *see also* Rocky Hill, N.J., Developmental Regulations Ordinance, § 704F(8), 713; Texas Historical Commission, Preservation Connection, *http://www.thc.texas.gov/public/upload/ forms/Texas%20 Statewide%20Preservation%20Plan%202011_2020.pdf.*

38 Alice E. Ingerson, What are cultural landscapes?, quoting the urban historian, Dolores Hayden, 1996, pp. 15, 21, 43, *http:// www.docsford.com/document/1142600.*

Chapter 9:
Adaptive Reuse

9A. Rehabilitating for Reuse

THE MILLS OF LOWELL, MASSACHUSETTS

Mills Museum at Lowell

Older cities are rich with historic properties—more than four thousand such city properties are listed on the National Register of Historic Places and even more may be eligible for listing. In recent economic declines, thousands of properties, a large percentage of which are defined as historic, have been vacated or gone into foreclosure, often leading to blighted conditions in neighborhoods that are home to residents who cannot or chose not to leave places to which they have a cultural, historical, economic, or social connection. As the case below illustrates, adaptive reuse may be the best response to these socio-economic phenomena.

Lowell, Massachusetts was a small industrial city thirty miles northwest of Boston. It was founded in the early 1820s as a planned town for the manufacture of textiles and named in honor of Francis Cabot Lowell. What was remarkable about the establishment was that it introduced a new system of integrated manufacturing to the United States and established new philosophies of employment and urban development that were soon replicated around New England and elsewhere. Only two decades after founding, the factories at Lowell employed and housed more than 8,000 textile workers, commonly known as mill girls or factory girls—primarily women and children from farming backgrounds. They were called "operatives" on account of their "operation" of the looms and other machinery. These jobs gave the mill girls a sense of freedom—from parental authority and economic dependence—earning their own way in the world and able to pursue educational opportunities. Although the hours were long, twelve-hour days, the mills routinely offered lectures after work or on weekends.[1]

By the 1850s, however, the Lowell system began to fail and it began using more and more immigrant and child labor, who were willing to work at very meager wages. As new technological advances made it easier and cheaper to manufacture textiles in the south, where cotton was grown locally, the labor was cheaper (fewer unions) and climate conditions more hospitable, textile manufacturing in New England started to decline in the 1890s. Rather than incorporate new technologies, the mills owners decided not to modernize or update their mills, instead they invested in building modern textile mills in the south. By the mid-20th century, all of the New England textile mills, including those at Lowell, had either closed or relocated to the south.

These business choices took their toll on the city of Lowell. Once the textile center of the nation, the city of 92,000 lost its economic infrastructure, leaving millions of square feet of mill space abandoned and deteriorating along rivers and canals. This important mill complex and many of the intact boarding

1 The Gilder Lehrman Institute of American History, The Gilder Lehrman Institute of American History, *https://www.gilderlehrman.org/content/lowell-mill-girls-and-factory-system-1840; see also* Dennis Frenchman and Jonathan S. Lane, *Discussion White Paper, Assessment of Preservation and Development in Lowell National Historical Park at its 30-Year Anniversary Where have we been and where should we be going?, http://citeseerx.ist.psu.edu/viewdoc/summary?doi=10.1.1.542.3662*; Lowell, Massachusetts, Report of the Lowell Historic Canal District to the Ninety-Fifth Congress of the United States of America, *https://home.nps.gov/lowe/learn/management/upload/1977_-Brown-Book-_reduced.pdf.*

houses—beautiful, substantial brick structures built in the fashion of the townhouses of Beacon Hill—were destroyed, replaced with open lots and dreary out-of-character buildings. As no new investment came to fill the void left by the shuttered mills, the city otherwise fell into decline—unemployment rose to the highest rate of any Massachusetts city and among the ten highest in the U.S. and the population plummeted.

Eschewing suggestions by planners and designers to use urban renewal funds to raze the whole community and start anew, the Lowell Historic Canal District Commission, later called the Lowell Historic Preservation Commission (LHPC), was formed with the mission of developing a better plan for the former mills.[2] With federal and state funds, the city rehabilitated three hundred structures. The LHPC provided over $5 million in preservation grants and loans for façade improvements. In addition to thirteen historic districts listed in the National Register of Historic Places, Lowell has two local architectural and design review districts. Approximately 78% of 5 million square feet of mill space in the District has been rehabilitated. It is now the Lowell National Historic Park.

The city has been revitalized as a tourist destination and improved place to live and work, aesthetically pleasing, with cultural events and education activities. A partnership between the University of Massachusetts at Lowell Graduate School of Education and the National Historical Park, the history center offers workshops and classroom materials on the life of the famous Lowell "mill girls" and other aspects of the textile-making industry.[3]

9A1. CAPTURING VALUE BY REHABILITATION AND REPURPOSING

Adaptive reuse means repurposing an existing building, while retaining and restoring as much of the original structural and passive aspects as possible. As an alternative to new construction, adaptive reuse serves the twin goals of historic preservation by revitalizing landmarks and the reduction of greenhouse gas emissions. Preserving an historic structure saves embodied energy, consumes less energy and produces less waste than new construction. Recycled

---

2 *https://www.lowellma.gov/575/Preservation-in-Lowell.*

3 *Id.*

projects are less costly, require less capital to start and take less time to complete.[4] Restored older buildings, such as late nineteenth-century warehouses, factories, and lofts, converted into desirable residential destinations for young adults and empty-nesters drawn to urban living, will cause other uses, including restaurants, entertainment destinations, and retail shopping, to follow. Unused property can be used for many other purposes, including greenways, forests, meadows, green infrastructure, and farms at different scales, all of which can enhance the quality of life in the city and region.

Traditionally, cities boast of walkable streets, well-developed infrastructure, public transit, dense employment centers, and rich social and cultural amenities. These amenities argue for allowing privately-owned historic buildings to be adaptively reused for affordable housing. Shrinking cities need density. Reconfiguring old buildings for multi-unit dwellings will increase density needed for thriving, vibrant neighborhoods. Abandoned or mothballed structures, including closed schools, old factories and industrial plants, churches, warehouses, mills, hotels, department stores, can be brought back to life for attractive and affordable housing or art galleries or restaurants.

Historic preservation by adaptive reuse responds to high development costs combined with limited development space, environmental costs and sustainability because abandoned industrial buildings can be purchased at prices substantially below replacement cost. Low acquisition costs, combined with available incentives and credits, can result in lease prices that are competitive with traditional office or industrial space or sales or rental prices the same or lower than residential market rates.

There are also aesthetic goals. The vernacular craftsmanship of historic industrial buildings is of a higher quality than most current construction. Industry long ago was driven by large and heavy machinery, so the floors were designed to withhold loads of 100 to 200 pounds per square foot. Many wall and floor

---

4 *See* Sheila Conejos, Craig Langston, Jim Smith, *Improving the Implementation of Adaptive Reuse Strategies for Historic Buildings, http://epublications.bond.edu.au/sustainable_development* (describing an Adaptive Reuse Potential Model for ranking adaptive reuse according to reuse potential that predicts useful life); Sara E. Sharpe, *Revitalizing Cities: Adaptive Reuse of Historic Structures, http://digitalcommons.wayne.edu/macaa2012scholarship/18* (describing case studies on successful adaptive reuse projects, including Ghirardelli Square in San Francisco, Baltimore Harbor, and Pittsburg Station Square).

surfaces were left exposed, which can save costs if that is part of the design aesthetic. Renovation of existing buildings can provide a green, environmentally friendly, and universally designed alternative to new construction as it provides an opportunity to bring an ancient building up to current codes and be more efficient. Retrofitting, using the existing structure, saves the cost of excavation, putting in foundations, footings, and structural systems. A community's built heritage and historic character, not found in newer construction, are preserved.

9B. LEED

Leadership in Energy and Environmental Design ("LEED") is a program created by the U.S. Green Building Council ("USGBC").[5] It is a rating system used for virtually all building, community and home project types and provides a framework for creating healthy, highly efficient and cost-saving green buildings. Historic buildings undergoing renovations or retrofits may qualify for certification under LEED for New Construction and Major Renovation (LEED-NC) or LEED for Existing Buildings: Operations & Maintenance (LEED-EBOM) rating systems respectively.[6] Another initiative, LEED for Neighborhood Development ("LEED-ND"), recognizes the benefits of historic preservation, in protecting and enhancing the overall health, natural environment, and quality of life of communities. Under LEED-ND, points are awarded to projects that incorporate smart growth principles and new urbanism design like walkable streets and mixed-use neighborhoods. While points are awarded for "Existing Building Reuse & Historic Building Preservation & Reuse," at the same time, no points are given if an historic building or portion of a historic building is demolished, unless demolition is approved by the local preservation review board. LEED-ND reflects the USGBC's growing understanding that historic preservation is a green building practice and a sustainable land-use policy.[7] LEED-ND integrates the principles of smart growth, new urbanism and green building, focusing on smart locations, alternative transportation modes, preservation of sensitive lands while discouraging sprawl. It features neighborhood design that emphasizes vibrant, diverse communities that are walkable, allows mixed-use; and incorporates

5 *https://new.usgbc.org/leed.*

6 *Id.*

7 *Id.*

design elements and construction that reduces energy and water consumption. Unlike the other LEED programs, LEED-ND is concerned not with the design of individual buildings, but with the connections between buildings and their context as well as the natural environment.[8] Projects pursuing LEED certification earn points across several categories, including energy use and air quality. Based on the number of points achieved, a project then earns one of four LEED rating levels: Certified, Silver, Gold or Platinum.[9]

9C. PRACTICAL AND REGULATORY OBSTACLES TO ADAPTIVE REUSE

Despite the clear societal and environmental benefits, there are yet political, legal and practical obstacles to adaptive reuse. There is the oft-expressed complaint that preservation impedes business development (but this is largely refuted by a number of studies that show increased vibrancy and property values in historic districts).[10] Deed restrictions may preclude changes in use and eliminating them is expensive and may be impossible under long-held property law rules. Regulatory barriers, such as building codes, environmental review and zoning ordinances may be daunting. Other impediments or barriers to adaptive reuse, such as neighborhood opposition, could cause delays in, or stop a project's implementation. Initial community opposition can also be experienced when developing a mixed-use or mixed-income housing project, even though such projects usually prove to be an asset to all concerned when development is completed. Site conditions may not be susceptible to adaptation. There could also be structural decay; obsolete and sometimes hazardous materials may need remediating at some cost.

Some cities have eliminated many of the practical obstacles. Los Angeles, for example, has an Adaptive Resource Ordinance[11] designed to facilitate the con-

8 *Id.*

9 *Id.*

10 *See e.g.*, Velma Zahirovic-Herbert and Swarn Chatterjee, Historic Preservation and Residential Property Values: Evidence from Quantile Regression, *http://citeseerx.ist.psu.edu/viewdoc/download?doi=10.1.1.906.1802&rep=rep1&type=pdf*; Vicki Been, Ingrid Gould Ellen, Michael Gedal, Edward Glaeser & Brian J. McCabe, *Preserving History or Hindering Growth? The Heterogeneous Effects of Historic Districts on Local Housing Markets in New York City*, National Bureau of Economic Research (Sept. 2014), *http:// www. nber. org/ papers/w20446.*

11 *http://www.downtownla.com/pdfs/econ_residential/Adaptive-Reuse-Book-LA.pdf.*

version of historic and underutilized structures into new housing units, by providing expedited approval and exemption from the zoning and code requirements that apply to new construction.[12] The ordinance encourages the conversion of the downtown's mostly historic office buildings into lofts, apartments, and hotels. In this regard, the ordinance does not require a building permit. Changing an industrial or a commercial building to a new residential use would normally require compliance with numerous rules and regulations, but the ordinance cuts through this red tape by streamlining the application process and providing significantly more flexibility in meeting building code and zoning requirements. Many non-compliant site conditions (including building height, parking, floor area and setbacks) are permitted without requiring a variance. Residential density requirements are also waived. New mezzanines less than one-third the floor area of the room below are not counted as floor area. The conversion of existing buildings to privately-owned residential use do not trigger disabled access requirements in the residential use area. Disabled access is still required in areas used by employees and that are open to the general public. The construction guidelines provide some flexibility in meeting structural and fire and life safety compliance requirements.

Portland, Oregon's zoning codes provides incentives to preservation, by transferring density or floor area ratio, allowing additional density for conversion in single-family zones to multiple unit dwellings, additional density in multi-unit dwelling zones, and providing exemptions from the minimum density requirements. It also allows non-residential uses in residential zones and increases the maximum parking ratios for historic properties in certain areas.[13] Boise, Idaho exempts historic properties from requirements of double-paned windows.[14]

The economic incentives include reduced tax rates, grants, and loans for restoration.[15] Under the Buffalo, N.Y.'s Adaptive Reuse Strategy, buildings at least 20 years old, vacant (50% or more) for at least 3 years and not generating significant

12 *www.preservation.lacity.org/incentives/adaptive-reuse-ordinances.*

13 *http://www.portlandoregon.gov/shared/cfm/image.cfm?id=150295.*

14 *www.cityofboise.org/media/85582/residential-historic-guidelines-4-8-14.pdf.*

15 *See e.g.*, Seattle's Incentives for Historic Preservation, Incentives for Historic Preservation, *https://historicseattle.org/advocacy/incentives/.*

rental income, are eligible for industrial development agency funding.[16] As a sustainable community is one that has sustainable plant life, more and more communities are creating urban agriculture districts and encouraging urban forests through new zoning and tax credits.[17] These uses work to preserve the natural landscapes of communities.

9D. NEW ZONING AND LAND USE MODELS

Historic preservation through adaptive reuse can work best under zoning ordinances that contain flexibility in permissible uses; significantly to allow mixed uses. This is the view taken by the Council on New Urbanism, which urges mixed uses that are not starkly incompatible toward creating livable and walkable communities.[18] Smart Codes and Form-Based Codes aim to restore urban centers in a coherent fashion that are designed for interaction with the physical environment and people. Streets should be designed to be walkable and accessible to transportation. Public spaces and public services should embrace community institutions and local history. Form-Based Codes focus on the form of buildings, their orientation, height, design, not their use. They aim to cause communities to grow around markers of history and remembrances and cultural assets, and embrace the urban landscape.[19] The urban historian, Witold Rybyzinski, has remarked that "[c]ities are man-made things, and because they are man-made, we can recognize a continuity of the ideas that went into their making."[20] These ideas include not only the grid layout for the facilitation of traffic and sale of lots, but also the spacing of houses and planting of trees for shade and beauty.[21] Adaptive reuse of buildings in their current orientation preserves those quaint ideas of community. A new urbanism is achieved by looking back.

---

16 *https://www.ecidany.com//adaptive-reuse.*

17 *See generally* Urban Agriculture: A Sixteen City Survey Of Urban Agriculture Practices Across the Country, *http://georgiaorganics.org/wp-content/themes/GeorgiaOrganics/Downloads/SiteMoveOver/urbanagreport.pdf*

18 Council for New Urbanism, *www.cnu.org_sites*; *http://www.newurbanism.org/sustainability.html*

19 *See* Form-Based Codes Institute, *https://formbasedcodes.org*; *see also* City of Sacramento, CA, Community Development Department, Planning, Urban Design, *Form Based Codes.*

20 Witold Rybczynski, City Life 50 (1996).

21 *Id.* at 79, 81. Despite some overarching ideas for city design, Rybczynski describes cities as organic, reflecting centuries of additions of different neighborhoods, gradually knitted together, growing by accretion. *Id.* at 46.

9E. SPECIAL BUILDING CODES

Some states have enacted dedicated historic building-specific codes. The Building Officials and Code Administrators (BOCA) and the International Conference of Building Officials (ICBO), the sources of many states' building codes, have adopted amendments to their model codes, to allow for alternative code solutions on historic preservation projects.[22] Adopting a rehabilitation code can cut costs for historic rehabilitation by up to 50 percent. California's State Historic Building Code ("CHBC"),[23] is an alternative code with building regulations and standards tailored specifically to the rehabilitation, preservation, restoration, relocation or change of occupancy of designated historic buildings. The CHBC aims to preserve original architectural elements and encourage cost-effective rehabilitation while also providing building safety. It does this by giving owners flexibility in finding economical methods to restore and retain integrity of the building's historic features. The CHBC exempts historical structures from certain requirements of the standard building code, allows wood roofing materials on a case by case basis, relaxes the requirements on the number of restrooms in a public facility, permits less efficient plumbing for toilets, includes special provisions for seismic retrofits, and protects historic properties from more stringent rules enacted by discretionary local authority.

New York's residential building code contains special provisions for historic structures.[24] The New Jersey State Uniform Construction Code—Rehabilitation Subcode, a chapter dedicated to historic buildings, is based upon the notion that historic buildings need not imitate new construction in every detail in order to be safe and accessible, allowing in the case of adaptive reuse, some changes in use, without bringing the structure into full compliance with the code. During the subcode's first year, rehabilitation work in New Jersey's five largest cities increased by 60 percent—with the vast majority of projects in Newark.

---

22 Building Codes and Historic Preservation: An Overview, Preservation Leadership Forum, *https://forum.savingplaces.org/viewdocument/building-codes-and-historic-preserv.*

23 CAL. HEALTH & SAFETY CODE, STATE HISTORICAL BLDG CODE, Part 2.7 §§18950, *et. seq.*.

24 Adopting Appendix J, 19 NYCRR parts 1219-1228 (residential building code). *See also* Maryland Building Rehabilitation Code, Article 12-1001, Public Safety.

9F. PARTNERSHIPS FOR REVITALIZATION: THE HISTORIC CEDAR-RIVERSIDE PLAZA

Cedar-Riverside Plaza, Minneapolis

The newly renovated Cedar-Riverside Plaza is a marvelous example of how communities and business can align for a successful adaptive reuse project that produces many radiating community benefits.

The boundaries of the Cedar-Riverside neighborhood were marked by interstate highways on the south and west and by the Mississippi River to the north and east. The University of Minnesota Twin Cities had its west campus there. Another college and a children's hospital also resided in the community. The rest of the neighborhood was occupied by commercial establishments and high-density residential properties. Riverside Plaza contained 1,303 apartments, which was 43 percent of all housing units in the community.

The first residents of Cedar-Riverside were German and Scandinavian immigrants, but over time, the population became predominantly East African and

East Asian. The presence of the institutions of higher education served the area well as approximately forty percent of residents were enrolled in college or graduate school. Despite high levels of education, poverty most characterized the area: 43 percent of households had an annual income of less than $10,000 (in 2012 inflation-adjusted dollars), 55 percent of all residents lived below the federal poverty level, and 15 percent of adult residents were unemployed.

The complex now known as Riverside Plaza was completed in 1974 as the first of 10 planned development projects to create a racially and socioeconomically integrated, mixed-use community, called Cedar Square West. Cedar Square West was the first of the new communities within urban areas, called "New Towns-In Town," to receive federal support under Title VII of the Housing and Urban Development Act of 1970. When community activists, led by the Cedar-Riverside Environmental Defense Fund, opposed further construction of the New Town-In Town, it left the project in a precarious financial position. Cedar Square West went into receivership in 1985, and HUD foreclosed the following year.

A group of investors led by Sherman Associates purchased the development in 1988, made structural repairs and other improvements, and renamed the property Riverside Plaza. Riverside Plaza required costly renovations to remain viable, including repairs to its failing electrical, mechanical, and plumbing systems. The Minnesota Historic Structure Rehabilitation Tax Credit, which had been recently approved by state lawmakers, opened up a potential source of funding that could make such extensive renovations possible, but this credit (as well as a federal historic tax credit)[25] was only available for rehabilitation of properties listed on the National Register of Historic Places. The property was eligible for the list based on its status as the first and larger of only two New Towns-In Town projects and for its architectural significance. The renowned Minnesota architect, Ralph Rapson, drew from European influences such as Le Corbusier's Unité d'Habitation, and incorporated distinctive design features into the project such as wood grain imprinted in the concrete and colorful exterior panels that were originally intended for tenants to decorate. The property is a monument to the 1970s federal urban development policy and embodies Rapson's Brutalist architectural style. Cedar Square West was listed on the National Register of Historic Places in December 2010.

---

25 Discussed below.

9F1. RENOVATION OF CEDAR SQUARE WEST

The renovation of the historic structure was extensive, including:

1. The electrical and mechanical systems

   Enhanced energy efficiency (25% reduction in consumption)

   New pipes; heating, ventilation, and air conditioning network

   Refurbished windows

   New patio doors

   Updated water system

2. Upgraded apartments and common areas

   Apartments' original design preserved

   90 percent of the units are affordable

   669 Section 8 units and an additional 505 units affordable to households earning less than 60 percent of the AMI

   The remaining 129 units market rate

   Varying sizes to the units:

   171 studio, 532 one-bedroom, 534 two-bedroom, 58 three-bedroom, and 8 four bedroom or larger apartments

3. Exterior and site improvements

   Sidewalks, fences, and handrails repaired or replaced.

   Repainting of the famous colored panels, returning them to their original bold hues

4. Neighborhood amenities

   Bicycle and pedestrian accessibility improved

   Renovation and expansion of the Cedar Riverside Community School—a K-8 charter school that has been housed in Riverside Plaza for more than 20 years.

   Improved lighting and signs, security cameras

   Improved cooperation between Riverside Plaza's owners and the Minneapolis Police Department, and a staffed safety center to address area crime concerns

5. Renewed community/connectivity/walkability

   Residents live just a short walk to light rail stations in all directions

The Hiawatha LRT bike trail runs through the neighborhood parallel to the Blue Line

6. Radiating effects

New light rail service, street improvements, and other housing developments nearby

9F2. FINANCING THE RENOVATION

The financing had many layers and components:

• A 4% Low-Income Housing Tax Credit	$29,106,637
• A HUD-Guaranteed First Mortgage	$49,950,000
• Federal Historic Tax Credits	$14,767,244
• State Historic Tax Credits	$14,126,603
• Minnesota Housing Finance Agency Economic Development and Housing Challenge	$7,016,350
• Minnesota Housing Finance Agency Preservation Affordable Rental Investment Fund	$5,083,650
• City of Minneapolis Affordable Housing Trust Fund	$1,900,000
• Greater Metropolitan Housing Corporation	$1,300,000
• Metropolitan Council Local Housing Incentives Account	$575,000
• Family Housing Fund	$200,000
• Deferred Developer Fee	$3,000,000
• Seller Equity	$2,000,000
• Cash Flow—Operations for total development costs	$2,962,909
• Energy Rebates from CenterPoint Energy and Xcel Energy	$400,000
• Hennepin County Environmental Response Fund	$150,000
• Metropolitan Council Tax Base Revitalization Account	$1,100,000

The total financing obtained: $133,638,393.[26]

26 Minneapolis, Minnesota: Preserving History and Affordable Housing in Cedar-Riverside, *https://www.huduser.gov/portal/casestudies/study_03032014_1.html.*

9G. FEDERAL AND STATE ECONOMIC INCENTIVES FOR REHABILITATION

Adaptive reuse is encouraged and supported by a host of federal and state tax and development incentives. The federal historic tax credit (HTC) provides a 20% credit, taken over five years, for expenditures for certified rehabilitation of income-producing historic properties, so long as the rehabilitation complies with the Secretary of Interior's Standards for the Treatment of Historic Property.[27] The a recent report on the program revealed that during the fiscal years 1978 through 2016, the HTC-related historic rehabilitation investment was more than $131.8 billion in inflation-adjusted 2016 dollars and in fiscal year 2016, that sum was about $6.5 billion, and producing more than 2.5 million jobs.[28]

Parallel state law credits, from 10 to 50%, can be used for owner-occupied residential properties, which have arguably suffered the most from vacancy and abandonment. Nearly two-thirds of the states have established state historic preservation tax credit programs[29] and like in Minnesota, many state and local economic development programs offer financial and business support. These programs (state and federal) can be deployed together and leveraged for remarkable results.[30]

Also available to assist in the rehabilitation of historic properties is the federal Low-Income Housing Tax Credit—9% per year for 10 years or 4% for

27 36 CFR §67.

28 *Annual Report on the Economic Impact of the Federal Historic Tax Credit for FY 2016, https://www.nps.gov/tps/tax-incentives/taxdocs/economic-impact-2016.pdf.*

29 *See https://www.novoco.com/resource-centers/historic-tax-credits/state-htcs/state-htc-program-descriptions.*

30 *See e.g.,* Annex: The Mills at High Falls, *https://www.preservenys.org/uploads/3/1/6/2/31626961/23537_annex_the_mills_at_high_falls_tax_credit_case_study_-_rochester.pdf.* For the conversion of an abandoned mill into modern apartments, the Rochester Economic Develop Corporation (ULREDC) combined its economic development and community revitalization efforts with resources from New York State's Homes and Community Renewal Agency (HCR), an organization that includes all the State's major housing and community renewal agencies under a single leadership and management structure to fund and manage projects. The City of Rochester committed funding to the project, initially to stabilize the buildings and undertake environmental testing and structural analysis. In addition to the federal and state tax credits, the project received loan funds from HCR's Housing Trust Fund Corporation. The ULREDC received a property tax exemption from the City of Rochester, with a 30-year annual payment in lieu of taxes (PILOT) agreement in the amount of 10% of its shelter rent (gross rents minus the cost of utilities).

property subsidized by tax-exempt bonds.[31] Historic Preservation Easements allow owners to ensure preservation of their property, with eligibility for an income tax deduction.[32] The Main Streets America Program[33] aims to revitalize and bring vibrancy to America's main streets for commerce and community. Federal funding is available to help with this initiative. Among other things, cities should assess street design for accessibility and navigability as well as parking requirements.

9H. THE COSTS OF PRESERVATION

Preservation involves choices: shore up and/rehabilitate an aging structure or raze it to construct some new, efficient and multi-purposed center. Federal and state government funding for preservation (for the purchase of structures and for rehabilitation) is not enough to defray all the upfront costs.[34] Consequently, preservation must rely on realizing investment in rehabilitation over the long-term. Federal government appropriations for historic preservation is still miserly, despite strong evidence that rehabilitation of historic structures contributes strongly to local GDP, in terms of jobs and commerce, and to housing.[35] It took a herculean effort by advocates to preserve the Historic Tax Credit in the

31 26 U.S.C. §42.

32 *See generally* Greg Mirza-Avakyan, *Adaptive Reuse of Historic Churches in New York City: the Opportunities and Challenges for Community Development*, Greg_Mirza-Avakyan_gam2137_Thesis.pdf; Donald J. Sevigny, *A Return to Manning the Post: the Adaptive Reuse of Publically Owned Fire Control Stations from the Second World War, http://docs.rwu.edu/hp_theses/2.*

33 *https://www.mainstreet.org/mainstreetamerica/themovement; see also Partners in Preservation: Main Streets2018, https://savingplaces.org/stories/partners-in-preservation-main-streets-2018#.W8cgo2hKg2w.*

34 Tax Cuts and Jobs Act of 2017, Pub. L. 115-97.

35 *Annual Report supra* note 28.

last Congress. But this was not the first time that the HTC was on the chopping block.[36] While it survives for now, is its fate certain?

Whether or not preservation has a higher claim to government support given the importance to the nation's posterity, it seems that it may never be a highly valued public priority, as compared to concerns about the opioid crisis, education, even the border wall. This may have something to do with labeling. Unfairly, preservation seems to be labeled as the cause of "liberals." This means that some line up for or against preservation initiatives based on the political label they assume. Strong property rights adherents are usually against local designation and claim the right to do what they will with their property. On the other side of the coin are those who believe that property carries limits derived from social obligations and these believers favor preservation. Weighing on the side of property rights are "takings" bills that restrict the regulatory authority of state and local governments that have been introduced in Congress and in nearly two dozen state legislatures.[37] And, in times of economic challenge, local governments continue as a matter of official policy to favor growth, jobs, and progress (a euphemism for tearing down all that is old and creating new). These circumstances portend fewer appropriations for preserving. Would a small tax (assessed to all property owners or included on sales) be a viable means of sustaining preservation efforts?

---

36 On November 2, 2017, the House of Representatives, without holding hearings, adopted H.R. 1, "Tax Cuts and Jobs Act," amendments to the Internal Revenue Code, within the procedures to adopt the nation's budget. The House bill entirely repealed the historic tax credit. The Senate's Committee on Finance reduced the credit from 20% to 10% and eliminated entirely the 10% tax credit for buildings built before 1936 which have not sought certification as historic. It was largely through the efforts of Senators Susan Collins (Maine) and Ben Cardin (Maryland) that in December 2017, at the last moment, Congress voted to preserve the tax credit, but with changes. The 20% credit must now be taken over five years, instead of in its entirety in the year the rehabilitation is completed. To be sure, this was not the first time that historic tax credits had been threatened, most recently, on December 11, 2014. Rep. Dave Camp (R. Mi.) introduced H.R. 1, "Tax Reform Act of 2014," which included the repeal of the credit. *See generally*, Stephanie Meeks and Kevin C. Murphy, The Past and Future City: How Historic Preservation is Reviving America's Communities (2016)(discussing the critical role that historic tax credits play in this revival).

37 The Private Property Protection Act, H.R. 1689, introduced by Rep. Jim Sensenbrenner (R-Wis.), would put strict limitations on the federal, state and local governments from exercising the power of eminent domain for economic development purposes *See generally,* Steven J. Eagle, *The Birth of the Property Rights Movement,* Cato Institute, Policy Analysis, December 2005.

Chapter 10:
Impact of Climate Change

The impacts of climate change represent a direct threat to all cultural heritage sites. These treats can be mitigated if emissions of greenhouse gases can be rapidly minimized. The means to do so exist.[1] Scientific models show how changes in Earth's atmosphere and temperatures are altering weather patterns. The United States National Academies of Science predict that "the magnitude and frequency of extreme climate and weather events are increasing, and sea level is rising along our coasts."[2] Landmarks and other cultural heritage sites face the kind of disruption and destruction that a storm surge and coastal tropical storm (no longer a hurricane) brought to New York City.

10A. Superstorm Sandy

More than 50 million people from the mid-Atlantic to New England were in Superstorm Sandy's path as it drove northward on a collision course with another storm system that was sweeping in from the west. The governors of New Jersey, Connecticut, Rhode Island, New York and Massachusetts all declared states of emergency and ordered residents in Sandy's likely path to evacuate. Thousands did, but many more did not. High winds and heavy rains were forecast. The impact would be major. Experts warned that even a diminished storm could wreak untold havoc because of the confluence of several weather systems that could lead to several feet of snow in West Virginia, Pennsylvania and Ohio, at the same producing wind and rain elsewhere. The approaching full moon promised greater flooding, with tides at their peak. Tens of thousands of National Guard troops in nine states were at the ready. The New York City subways were shut and bridges would be closed if there were sustained winds over 60 miles

---

1 Michael B. Gerrard and John C. Dernbach, Legal Pathways to Deep Decarbonization In the United States (Environmental law Institute, 2019).

2 National Academies of Sciences, Engineering, and Medicine, at *http://sites.nationalacademies.org/sites/climate/index.htm.*

per hour. The mayor of New York closed the city parks. The governor of New Jersey warned residents to expect power outages and that it could be seven to ten days before electricity would be restored. Amtrak stopped its Washington, D.C. to New York route. Airports closed. The stock markets went dark.[3]

Sandy's hit was severe. The human cost was gargantuan: 147 killed; thousands of homes destroyed or rendered unlivable (110 homes burned to the ground in one Queens community). The damage was estimated to top $71 billion. The nearly fourteen feet ocean surge and thirty-two feet waves ravaged the coast line. While the Statue of Liberty still stood when Sandy abated, other historic structures that could not evacuate or resist Sandy's forces were hit hard. The Fraunces Tavern, a gathering place for revolutionary war-era patriots (George Washington, Alexander Hamilton, John Adams) flooded and the electrical system corroded from salt water intrusion. The Palmer Tennis House in Rye, the third oldest indoor court in the country lost its roof and its truss system weakened. Green-Wood Cemetery, a National Historic Landmark and the resting place of many luminaries (Leonard Bernstein, Horace Greeley, eight victims of the Triangle Shirtwaist Factory Fire) lost many trees and had damage to the Breithaupt Mausoleum. The Lehigh Valley Barge, the only surviving all-wooden example of the Hudson River Railroad Barge, saw ripped planking, walkways and sheathing. Lookout Hill, a centerpiece of the 1870 Prospect Park, designed by Fredrick Law Olmsted and Calvert Vaux (who also designed New York City Central Park) lost more than 500 trees and suffered severe damage to wooded slopes. The historic South Street Seaport was all but disintegrated.[4]

---

3 By Marc Santora, Urgent Warnings as Hurricane Sandy Heads to Northeast, *https://www.nytimes.com/2012/10/28/us/hurricane-sandy-on-collision-course-with-winter-storm.html.*

4 *See Governor Cuomo Announces $6.2 Million in Grants for Historic Properties Damaged By Superstorm Sandy, https://www.governor.ny/gov/news/governor-cuomo-announces-62-million-grants-historic-properties-damaged-superstorm-sandy; see also* Office of the Mayor, *A Stronger, More Resilient New York,* PlaNYC 373-74, 376 (2013), *available at http://s-media.nyc.gov/agencies/sirr/SIRR_singles_Lo_res.pdf.* Hurricane Katrina was disastrous to the historic city of New Orleans. About one-fifth of New Orleans' urban area is in an historic district listed on the National Register of Historic Places. It was the single largest disaster for cultural resources in the United States since the National Historic Preservation Act of 1966 was enacted. Hurricane Katrina in the Gulf Coast Mitigation Assessment Team Report, *http://www.fema.gov/media-library-data/20130726-1520-20490-4521/549_ch8.pdf.*

10B. THE IMPERATIVES OF CLIMATE CHANGE

Climate change presents numerous threats to historic properties—from more frequent and intense droughts, more severe storms, more flooding, longer heat waves, and rising sea levels.[5] The leading experts are warning that the planet's fragile ecological balance could be irrevocably disturbed if the activities fueling climate change go unabated. The threat to heritage and cultural properties is particularly worrisome. Historic properties are more vulnerable to these effects because they are old, unfortified and situated near the coast. Ancient buildings that were designed in a climate less malevolent may not be able to tolerate significant changes. Severe flooding and increases in storms, along with melting permafrost threaten to unearth buried archaeological evidence. Sea level rise and coastal erosion will engulf cultural heritage sites located in coastal lowlands.[6] Increases in soil moisture and salt absorbed through the porous structures leading to crystallization will destabilize precariously situated structures. Increased infestation of timber and other organic building materials by pests migrating from other altitudes and latitudes, will cause them to topple.[7]

The Intergovernmental Panel on Climate Change ("IPCC"), established under the auspices of the World Meteorological Organization (WMO) and the United Nations Environment Programme (UNEP), issues periodic assessment reports that synthesizes all relevant evidence of climate change.[8] Greenhouse effect, the trapping of energy (particularly, carbon dioxide (CO_2) molecules) radiated by the Earth into the atmosphere, instead of escaping into outer space, has been identified as the main driver of climate change. Since the Industrial Revolution, CO_2 concentration has risen to more than 379 ppm. Global average temperatures have risen by more than 0.6 ($\pm$ *0.2*)℃ over the twentieth century. There has been widespread retreat of mountain glaciers in non-polar regions; a decrease in spring and summer sea-ice by 10% to 15% in the Northern Hemisphere since the

---

5 *See* IPCC Fifth Assessment, *https://www.ipcc.ch/report/ar5/syr/.*

6 *Id.*

7 Susan Shearing, *Here Today, Gone Tomorrow? Climate Change and World Heritage*, Macquarie University 2007 at 9.

8 *https://www.ipcc.ch/about/.*

1950s; a rise in global ocean heat content since the late 1950s; and rising global average sea levels by at least 0.1 m during the twentieth century.[9]

The last IPCC projections are equally alarming: by 2100, atmospheric CO_2 concentrations will reach 540 to 970 ppm; global average surface temperature will increase by 1.4°C to 5.8°C from 1990 to 2100; global mean sea levels will rise by 0.09m to 0.88m between 1990 and 2100; and global average water vapor concentration and precipitation will increase. It is expected that changes in extreme and/or severe weather events such as heat waves, droughts, extreme precipitations, severe tropical cyclones, will also occur. The IPCC warns that unless rises in global temperatures are kept at or below 1.5°C, global sea level rise will be at astronomical levels and oceans free of sea ice will occur once per decade as opposed to once per century.[10]

10C. CLIMATE CHANGE AND WORLD HERITAGE

There are some 890 World Heritage Sites.[11] They are so designated because they are regarded as irreplaceable sources and reflections of human existence and inspiration; they are timeless in serving as a bridge between the past and future. They are both man-made (the Great Wall) and natural (the Grand Canyon). They are equally exposed to the ravages of climate change.[12] The recently-published Case Studies on Climate Change and Cultural Heritage, highlights several cases of the impact of climate change on specific heritage sites: the Sagarmatha National Park in Nepal (melting glaciers); Great Barrier Reef in Australia (rising ocean temperatures retarding the growth of coral); Wet Tropics of Queensland, Australia (rising temperatures threatening ability of species to adapt); Golden Mountains of Altai, Russian Federation (floods, melting glaciers); the City of London and Venice (persistent high tides, storm surges).[13]

9 IPCC Fifth Assessment, *supra* note 3.

10 AR5 Synthesis Report: Climate Change 2014, *https://www.ipcc.ch/sr15/*.

11 *https://whc.unesco.org/en/list/*.

12 Case Studies on Climate Change and Cultural Heritage, whc.unesco.org_uploads_activities_documents_activity-473-1.pdf; *see also* UCL Centre for Sustainable Heritage, Climate Change and the Historic Environment, May Cassar, *http://discovery.ucl.ac.uk/2082/1/2082.pdf, www.ucl.ac.uk/sustainableheritage/climatechange/climatechangeandthehistoricenvironment.pdf.*

13 *whc.unesco.org_uploads_activities_documents_activity-473-1.pdf.*

The "threatening effects of climatic, geological or other environmental factors" has become a driver for the inscription of properties on the List of World Heritage in Danger. The threatening effects may be gradual, incremental or sudden and call for corrective measures to address both the threats and their deleterious effects on properties. In some cases, it may not be possible to correct the threats by human action (in the case of extreme weather events) while action can be taken to deal with their deleterious effects. Because climate related threats are beyond the control of any individual state party, nations where heritage is situated, may be relegated to implementing adaptation measures (adjustments to our ways of living and use of heritage property to moderate harm, and only limited mitigation measures (human intervention to reduce the sources or enhance the sinks of greenhouse gases).[14]

10D. DOMESTIC RESPONSES TO CLIMATE CHANGE

Both adaptation and mitigation measures have been deployed to contain or at least slow the progress of climate change. Unprecedented sums for disaster relief, mitigation and adaption have been spent and are planned to be spent by the federal and state governments in fighting climate change.[15]

There are legions of toolkits, guides and prescriptions prepared by think tanks,[16] offering materials for resiliency and sustainability.[17] Private industry and trade associations have embraced the concept of sturdier construction of buildings.[18]

---

14 *World Heritage in Danger: A compendium of key decisions on the conservation of natural World Heritage properties via the List of World Heritage in Danger*, (IUCN, 2008).

15 Shelby D. Green, *Building Resilient Communities in the Wake of Climate Change While Keeping Affordable Housing Safe From Sea Changes in Nature and Policy*, 54 Washburn L.J. 527, 551; (2015) Shelby D. Green, *Zoning Neighborhoods for Resilience: Drivers, Tools and Impacts*, 28 Fordham Envtl L. Rev. 41 (2016).

16 Green, Resilience, *supra* note 15, at 67-68.

17 *Id.*

18 The Institute for Business & Home Safety ("IBHS") promulgated fortified building standards for resiliency to all events, including winds and wildfires, such as dry floodproofing (using seals, veneers, film); wet floodproofing (employing flow through mechanisms); structural design to withstand winds; elevation of appliances, furnace, water heater, compressor, and electrical systems; sturdier roof structures, secondary barriers, and improved connections between roof and structural materials. INSTITUTE FOR BUSINESS & HOME SAFETY 5 (2008), *http://www.disastersafety.org/wp-content/uploads/fortified-safer-living-standards_IBHS.pdf.*

Cities are requiring,[19] and others are encouraging,[20] resiliency and sustainability measures. Hundreds have adopted climate action plans, climate mitigation plans and/or resiliency plans; some carrying out state mandates;[21] others under their own local land use powers.[22] To blunt the effects of strong winds, and earth quakes, cities have updated building codes to require fortifications—some adopting FEMA's standards, others developing their own.[23] To protect against the crippling effects of flooding, cities are requiring elevations (of sites, structures, and critical systems), the use of wind and water resistant materials,[24] fire safe design and emergency back-ups.[25] To help hold back the encroaching seas, cities are also fortifying public infrastructure, elevating roads and bridges, installing permeable pavements and green alleys,[26] utilizing buffers and setbacks from sea shores.[27] To contain greenhouse gases, cities are adopting measures on energy usage,[28] aiming for energy efficiency from a number of different angles

---

19 Elizabeth C. Black, *Climate Change Adaptation: Local Solutions for a Global Problem*, 22 Geo. Int'l Envtl. L. Rev. 359, 378 (2010)(discussion the two primary tracks that cities could use in accomplishing these dual goals of increasing green space and encouraging green building. "Carrots" include tax incentives, grants and fee waivers, expedited permitting and density bonuses. "Sticks include zoning and building code requirements.

20 *Id.* at 380-82.

21 California Climate Action Plan, www.climatechange.ca.gov; NYC 2100 Commission, *www.rebuildbydesign.org/research/resources/36-resources/70/70.*

22 *See e.g.*, Chicago Climate Task Force, *Chicago Climate Action Plan* (2008), *http://www.chicagoclimateaction.org/*; San Diego Climate Action Plan, *https://www.sandiego.gov/planning/genplan/cap*; PlaNYC, *http://www.nyc.gov/html/planyc/html/resiliency/resiliency.shtml* (multifaceted guide, covering housing, transport, solid waste, heating oils); *see generally*, U.S. Conference of Mayors, Taking Local Action: Mayors and Climate Protection Best Practices 5 (2014), *http://usmayors.org/climateprotection/2014awardees/0620-report-climateprotectionbp.pdf; See generally, FEMA Hazard Mitigation Guide, http://www.fema.gov/media-library/assets/documents/31372*; Georgetown Climate Center, 20 Good Ideas, *www.georgetownclimate.org* ("20 Good Ideas").

23 *See generally* Green, *supra* note 15.

24 URB. GREEN COUNCIL, *Building Resiliency Task Force*, 14 (2013), *http://issuu.com/urbangreen/docs/brtf_executive_summary.*

25 PlaNYC, *supra* note 20, at 126, 129 (hookups for access to generators, anti-backflows, and faucets in common areas).

26 Erika Spanger-Siegried, et al., *Encroaching Tides: How Sea Level Rise and Tidal Flooding Threaten U.S. East and Gulf Coast Communities over the Next 30 Years*, Union of Concerned Scientists, (Oct. 2014), available at *http://www.ucsusa.org/sites/default/files/attach/2014/10/encroaching-tides-full-report.pdf.*

27 Encroaching Tides, *supra* note 26 at 7, 13, 14 (steep slope mountain ridge protection; maximum grading allowances; preservation of green space).

28 *See* New York State Energy Planning Bd., *The Energy to Lead: 2015 New York State Energy Plan* 18-23, 69-77 (2015), *http://energyplan.ny.gov/.*

including: new standards, the most common of which is the LEED standard;[29] adopting requirements for reflective coatings, green and cool roofs;[30] supporting energy star qualified homes;[31] encouraging geothermal, solar and wind energy;[32] using low-impact hydro-power, alternative fuels and smart grids;[33] and setting up green banks.[34] Transportation systems are being upgraded and cities are investing in measures to facilitate less polluting means of transportation; installing charging stations for electric cars;[35] and facilitating biking and walking as desirable modes of transportation.[36]

Some of these measures may not be feasible for historic properties. Seawalls go only so far to keep out 14-foot storm surges and 32-foot waves. Elevating an historic structure may change its character-defining context; the new stilts mocking its original stance and rendering them inaccessible to the many unable to climb. Putting in new roofs and energy efficient windows may turn an historic cottage into a modern building. In historic preservation, significance and

29 Leadership in Energy and Environmental Design (LEED). The city of Atlanta requires all city-funded projects over 5,000 square feet or over $2 million dollars meet LEED Silver standard. *Resilient Atlanta: Action to Build an Equitable Future, https://issuu.com/resilientatlanta/docs/100rc_strategy-document_withcover.*

30 To reduce the urban heat island effect, Chicago will add 6,000 buildings with cool roofs by 2020, which is expected to reduce temperatures by average of 7 degrees. Chicago Climate Action Plan, *supra* note 20, at 22.

31 *See Learn how Portfolio Manager helps you save,* ENERGYSTAR, *http://www.energystar.gov/buildings/facility-owners-and-managers/existing-buildings/use-portfolio-manager/learn-how-portfolio-manager.*

32 Cal. Pub. Resources Code §25980 (striving to balance the interest in solar panels against shade from trees, Trees must be allowed to stand. Pub. Res. Code § 25980, 25984 (trees planted before the installation of solar collectors are protected). Homes must be removed from flood prone areas. LOCAL GOV'TS FOR SUSTAINABILITY USA, LOCAL GOVERNMENTS, EXTREME WEATHER AND CLIMATE CHANGE 2012 5 (2012), *available at http://www.resilientamerica.org/wp-content/uploads/2013/06/ICLEI_extreme_weather_cities_fact_sheet_2012.pdf.* (describing plan adopted in King County, Washington to demolish chronically flooded homes); City of Phoenix, Ariz., *City adopts new goal to reduce greenhouse gas (GHG) emissions from city operations to 15 percent by 2015, https://www.phoenix.gov/oep/environment/climate.*

33 Green Cincinnati Plan 2013 (planned net-zero police station), in INT'L COUNCIL FOR LOCAL ENVTL. INITIATIVES & WORLD WILDLIFE FUND, MEASURING UP 2015: HOW U.S. CITIES ARE ACCELERATING PROGRESS TOWARD NATIONAL CLIMATE GOALS 35 (2015), available at *https://www.worldwildlife.org/stories/measuring-up-2015-how-us-cities-are-accelerating-progress-toward-national-climate-goals.*

34 *Id.* at 8.

35 2014 Cal. Stats. ch. 529.

36 City of Portland, in Measuring Up, *supra* note 33, at 20, 26 (calling for bike paths/lanes, walkability; already there are more than 300 miles of bikeways).

integrity of a resource are regarded as largely fixed once they have been assessed and determined; however, each site's significance should be "seen as time bound and in need of periodic revision...The essential nature of significance...[is] an expression of cultural meaning, it must be expected to change, involve multivalence and contention, and be contingent on time, place, and other factors."[37]

In the end, documenting the historic site, as is often required before a demolition is allowed under state and local preservation laws, or where possible, removal to a new site, may be the only recourse. Some things were built for all time and will be able to withstand mother nature's angriest expression, others will succumb. The Statue of Liberty, one of our greatest landmarks, remains as a beacon to humanity.

10E. THE JAY PROPERTY AND ENVIRONMENTAL CHANGE

The fate of the historic Jay Property landscape is not entirely to be decided by the decisions of the JHC or County Parks or any other interested party. We now live in the Anthropocene epoch, in which humans are altering the natural cycles of the Earth. The impacts of climate change alter the hydrologic cycle, inducing in turn periods of more rainfall as well as periodic drought and extreme weather events. Impacts from human development crowd out other species, producing a thinning in the numbers of species, reducing habitat and impeding migration, and accelerating rates of extinction. Sea level rise is reshaping coastlines.

The Jay Property is well-positioned to serve society amidst this era of environmental change. The Jays chose the site for The Locusts along the top of a ridge. When Peter Augustus Jay rebuilt the present Greek Revival Mansion, it incorporated the materials of the earlier farm house, and enjoyed the same natural benefits of the site. All rain waters naturally flow away from the building. It features a back porch facing east toward Long Island Sound, with a central door and windows the full height of the wall of the two parlor rooms. This permits the cool air from the Long Island Sound to rise up and flow into the house, and through the hallway out the front door. The Mansion has natural air conditioning. The

37 Randall Mason, "Fixing Historic Preservation: A Constructive Critique of 'Significance,'" *Places, A Forum of Environmental Design* 16.1 (2004): 64-65.

house was built to withstand all weather conditions and has survived many hurricanes. Its resilient construction offers design insights.

When the Methodist Church owned the Peter Jay Mansion, it installed a forced air heating and cooling system. Rather than reactivate this, the JHC decided to install geothermal wells in the roadway adjacent and provide natural cooling and heating for the Mansion. The JHC has adopted standards for sustainably caring for its site.[38] The site produces few greenhouse gases, and because it is accessible by the Boston Post Road, it could have a transportation policy favoring access by public electric buses as these mass transit options become workable. The JHC is well positioned in terms of mitigating climate change.

Springs rise slightly down hill from the Peter Jay Mansion, and the site is well served by naturally flowing fresh waters. At the base of the ridge to the west is the coast of Long Island Sound. Sea level rise is gradually inundating small islands all along the Sound, but the sea level sites where Jay's shipping would have docked are some fifty feet in elevation below the carriage paths that led from his piers uphill to the Mansion, along the meadow. Even the coastal rocks, left by the glaciers, that still hold the mortars the indigenous people used, are well above the rising coasts. Because the Jay Property's pathways to the sea are easily accessed, they can measure and teach about sea level rise. Perhaps access to the site will once again also be by sea, as well as by the Boston Post Road.

To study the impacts of climate change, it is important to have large natural areas, where long-term changes in flora and fauna are possible. The 3000-year meadow awaits systematic study of its baseline conditions, now and in the past, so that one can assess ecological change in the future. All other ecological aspects of the entire Jay/Marshlands acres offer opportunities to document environmental change over time. Since these are "preserved" places, scientific study can be maintained without loss of access for multi-year periods. The Jay/Marshlands habitats can be enhanced to assist in species migration, and foster biodiversity. Since these acres are enclosed on three sides by suburban homes, environmental studies can also address exploring measures to enhance the ambient environment in the midst of this type of land use.

38 Jay Heritage Center, "Stewardship Through Smart Choices" (2017), *https://jayheritagecenter.org/visit/buildings-grounds/stewardship-through-smart-choices.*

Beyond sharing a Cultural Heritage Report for the Jay Property and Marshlands Conservancy to guide stewardship of these lands, they share a common fate. The types of land uses, and the density of development permitted by the City of Rye has produced an anomaly. This site is now an "island." It is offering a refuge for some wildlife, but also a prison for others. The white tail deer population has no place to go, and deer threaten the restoration of gardens at the Jay Property as well as wild flora in Marshlands. The JHC has removed invasive vines and other species that shrouded historic features. What is the measure of ecological health appropriate to the County's nature conservancy? How will stewards in the future come to better manage this biological and cultural island overlooking Long Island Sound?

More problematic are the issues of recovery after an intensive storm. What options for restoration or adaptive reuse exist, and what criteria should guide those choices? In time, the JHC will develop an Adaptation Policy to address such issues.

The legacy of John Jay's home in Rye is a many faceted one. Each generation is likely to contest it anew.

Chapter 11: Sustaining Public Investment in Cultural Heritage

America has made the investments, both public and private, in securing its cultural heritage. How likely it is that the nation can sustain these sunk costs and ongoing disbursements? It pays for us now to speculate about the future of our commitments to the past.

11A. Whither Historic Preservation?

Not everyone supports historic preservation. There are strong economic interests that seek development of real estate regardless of the history of the property they control. For some, creating a new landmark is more essential than worrying about the architecture of the past. For others, regulation of "private property" is opposed in principle and an intrusion on individual liberty. The priorities of some find it convenient to exclude care for history, so a hospital must attend to those in need and not divert funds to its own historical heritage, or a university must attend to its educational mission before devoting scarce income to expensive restorations of older buildings. A wilderness proponent may not wish to keep an obsolete fire tower in the Adirondacks or an abandoned mine in a federal wilderness. A church may need its funds to serve its flock and its faith, rather than repair the roof of a landmark it owns. An environmentalist may have little patience for saving an energy-inefficient art deco building on a site needed for new solar panels, or conversely the wind farm proponent may not care about how the wind turbines affect viewsheds or migratory species.

Although the broad contours of historic preservation law are well-settled across America, these sorts of controversies persist. These are competing interests. Not everyone shares the same stories about their past or values the stories of those with other memories not their own. Preservation law is very much about the procedures that are appropriate to identify, listen to, build mutual understanding, and seek to resolve competing perspectives. When this is not possible, preservation law has developed rules that resolve the contending claims.

When a local government adopts a preservation ordinance, it makes a fundamental legislative choice about the process to safeguard its cultural heritage. State legislatures have done so in authorizing their local governments to adopt these sorts of local laws. State legislatures instruct their own agencies about how to protect historic structures that they own. The Congress has done so with federal land and structures, through the Antiquities Act, the NHPA and other statutes. In the past century, preservation law has emerged as a product of individual policies at all levels of government across most of America.

The apparently settled body of law described in this book *will* further evolve for several reasons. One is remarkable and secular. New technological innovations exist to document, care for, or harm cultural and natural heritage. How will artificial intelligence be deployed to further or frustrate restoring an historic site? A second phenomenon is the populist disruption of traditional political patterns. Will a revolted politics change the democratic consensus for historic preservation? Third, the disruptions of climate change may be infinitely worse than now projected, and as communities face existential threats, will they have time for protecting their cultural heritage?

11B. CHANGING TOOLS VIA TECHNOLOGICAL INNOVATION

While local preservation laws moved in the late 1960s to 1980s from being exotic to being common place, the Internet was just emerging, and had no role to play in establishing the foundational laws for stewardship of cultural heritage. The Internet has become essential to applying and elaborating presevation programs. Remote sensing was just beginning to be used by landscape planners and preservation professionals. Photographic drones to film, map and record landscapes had not been invented or deployed. Cognitive technologies, though rapidly developing, with algorithms and software codes reshaping how data is assembled and accessed and mined, had not matured to predictable uses. Big data had not emerged. Problem-solving "hackathons" were only a few years old. Now, "virtual reality" video systems record and headsets enable anyone to visit a physical historic structure without being there, or without the structure even still existing.

It was once essential to require architects to prepare measured drawings of landmark buildings slated for demolition. Photographs were used to identify the façades of structures for landmark designation reports, placed in hard copy paper file, but few municipal budgets could afford many such photographs. Now, technologies to permit comprehensive digital photographs are readily available and can be loaded onto databases and easily retrieved when needed. Arial images can be had at many scales, taken from drone or satellites.[1] Within the National Park Service, the Cultural Resources Geographic Information Systems facility (CRGIS) is a program "dedicated to developing and fostering the use of geographic information systems (GIS) and global positioning systems (GPS) technologies in documenting, analyzing and managing cultural resources." Among other things, CRGIS helps to identify management issues, assess historic significance and to understand the context in which cultural significance is assessed.[2]

Cultural preservation in Europe is today beginning the task of compiling electronic databases of cultural heritage[3] at risk to sea level rise or flooding or fire, such as the recent damage to the Cathedral Notre Dame.[4]

1 *http://npshistory.com/publications/interdisciplinary/gis/fs-gis.pdf*

2 For two decades, CRGIS has worked to institutionalize GIS and GPS as an essential tool in cultural resource management, using these technologies for field surveys and inventory maintenance, along with establishing links between cultural resource databases using locational information. CRGIS works with State/Tribal Historic Preservation Offices, local agencies, preservation organizations, universities and other Federal agencies, providing technical services and training in these technologies to specific cultural resource management projects, to learn how to identify cultural resources management issues and to provide a better and more dynamic access to resources. CRGIS has been used to document engineering features and structures to large landscapes and traditional cultural properties; to help inventory cultural resources from battlefields to cemeteries, to develop strategies to identify and evaluate affected properties following severe weather events, helping to evaluate their historic significance in compliance with historic preservation laws. CRGIS technology can be used to understand the context within which resources acquire significance. National Park Service, Cultural Resources Geographic Information Systems (CRGIS), *https://www.nps.gov/crgis/.*

3 *See Marie Curie Initial Training Network on Digital Cultural Heritage, supra* Chapter 4, note 40.

4 On April 15, 2019, the roof of the Cathedral Notre Dame, while undergoing renovations, caught fire. The cathedral suffered serious damage, including the spire and most of the lead-covered wooden roof above the stone vaulted ceilings. The cathedral was named a World Heritage Site in 1991 and was widely accepted as one of the finest examples of French Gothic architecture. Construction began in 1160 and was not completed for another century. It was estimated that it will take fifteen years to restore. But, restoration might not be possible at all, but for the foresight of an architectural historian, who in 2015, created exacting 3D laser scans of the cathedral. *See* Adam Rogers, *The Notre Dame Fire and the Future of History,* Science, *https://www.wired.com/story/the-notre-dame-fire-and-the-future-of-history/.*

Artificial Intelligence (AI) has the techniques to identify and match up local preservationists with comparable interests. Finding a site and local sponsors that could receive a landmark removed before it is inundated and destroyed, is now possible. Even though the future of cultural heritage stewardship may depend on creating a new AI dimension to cultural heritage stewardship and the development of such technologies is accelerating, these technologies are not yet widely available or affordable to local preservationist groups.

11C. CHANGING POLITICS: IS HISTORIC PRESERVATION IN THE PRESENT?

What does populism in American political life portend. Is reverence for the old a thing of the past? Has the immediacy of the internet made history irrelevant? Is there new culture being created that is worthy of protection? Why should we protect when many fail to see any value in it? What is preservation's value to and place in contemporary life? The joinder of preservation efforts in a coordinated educational effort on a continuing basis, that focuses on the larger preservation ethic rather than on individual organizations or threatened resources, might be a step toward growing and sustaining public investment in the cause.

A greater emphasis on a broad range of unfamiliar and diverse associative values, as well as appreciation for urban and rural development patterns and new design concepts will serve to encourage buy-ins as they create a better connection to citizen input.[5] Heritage areas must be integrated into the day-to-day activities of and closely associated with the private and non-profit sectors. Adaptive reuse projects must be encouraged and supported and successes publicly celebrated. More coherence, a stronger guiding statement of policy that is understood by and resonant to laypeople should be pursued. A bottom-up, consumer-oriented structure rather than a top-down aggregation of national organizational interests should be embraced. Perhaps another Conference of United States Mayors should update WITH HERITAGE SO RICH, moving historic

5 *See* Seth M. Low, "Cultural Conservation of Place," in *Conserving Culture: A New Discourse on Heritage*, ed. Mary Hufford 1994.

preservation forward in a united fashion. "Life is change. You cannot avoid or outrun change no matter where you go."[6]

Gary Machlis and Jonathan Jarvis, both career leaders of the National Park Service, offer some perspective on the changes that populism promotes in America today: "As the wave of populist anger and resentment bears down on the national laws and policies that protect the environment, there is an inclination in the conservation community to veer haphazardly from cautious hope to indecisive despair."[7] Among the strategies they urge to navigate begween these extremes is to "Connect all citizens to American nature, history and culture through first-hand experience."[8] They urge an expansion of protected areas and the integration of cultural and natural heritage. They are two both human endeavors, based on appreciation of heritage and when united they mutually reinforce each other. In their words:

> Strategic expanson of protected areas should be a prority at every level, and advocates should build broad support beyond the traditional conservation community. Many of America's mayors are recognizing that parks, riverfronts and lakefronts, greenways, tree canopy, and other outsdoor recreation sites attract new companies and are keys to a livable city. There is increasing evidence that green infrastruture contributes to crime reduction, pubic health, water quality, storm protection, reduced energy consumption and the social fabric of a community.[9]

The story of saving John Jay's property in Rye offers confirmation of what Machlin and Jarvis observe. Preservationists and conservationist share the same administrative legal landscape. They rely on the same laws and ultimately on shared public support for heritage. In the face of populist disruption to the political system, new grassroots alliances are needed to rebuild the political landscape. In their view, "Nature conservation organizations and historic preservation groups share little in the way of strategies, tactics, or resources

---

6 Leah Hager Cohen, Strangers and Cousins 266 (2019).

7 Gary E. Machlis and Jonathan B. Jarvis, The Future of Conservation in America—A Chart for Rough Water 42 (2018).

8 *Id.* at p. 48.

9 *Id.* at p. 54.

and often (as in lawsuits by wilderness advocates to remove historic structures) actively oppose each other."[10] The time has come to forge a "more unified vision" of heritage conservaton. The Jay Heritage Center points the way to do so.

11D. CHANGING CLIMATES: RADICAL REFORMS OF PRESERVATION AGENDAS AND APPROACHES

This book has described the well-accepted and settled legal and administrative practices that characterize historic preservation law today in America. It has taken decades to reach this point, but it is a mistake to assume that it follows a linear trajectory toward refining and enhancing the systems described above. As Chapter 10 on Climate Change makes plain, the impacts of climate change ultimately alter everything.

Consider the historic sites in the Southwestern arid states. Changes in the hydrologic cycle may bring less rainfall to this region. Was an earlier prolonged drought the reason the Anasazi abandoned their pueblos? The ancient sites in Chaco Canyon have been kept dry and naturally "preserved" for centuries before federal historic preservation laws protected them from human interference. Cultural heritage sites and structures on the National Register of Historic Places can be secured when local residents move out, but what standards should be applied to conserve these places? Will anyone inspect them? How will future tourism be accommodated? Can "ghost town" landscapes adequately present and enable interpretive conservation of historic structures?

11D1. *EX SITU* PRESERVATION

The largest numbers of historic buildings and sites are found along the nation's sea coasts. It was here that immigrants first settled and remained. The sites are at risk to immediate threats from more extreme storms and rising sea levels. Wind-driven storm surges inundate areas at elevations, which are at or near sea level, often quite far inland. In the last inter-glacial period, the coastlines of North America were many leagues from today's coasts. Human settlements now populate this coastal plain, and vast parts of it will probably face inundation in

10 *Id.* at p. 69.

the coming century or more. There is ample warning and time to prepare. The National Register properties can be inventoried in terms of the likely risks of their threatened destruction, and measures taken to record or dismantle and either store or exhibit in museums or inland site such as in Sturbridge Village, Massachusetts, where historic buildings dating from the 1790s to the 1830s have been relocated and reassembled in an imagined New England village setting.[11] What standards should apply to distinguish such salvaging of cultural heritage from creating a new "Disneyland." If funds are limited for the tasks, how will they be allocated and what is the fate of structures which cannot be saved in time?

River Valleys are also home to many historic sites and structures. They were the highways of the nation for two centuries and still serve that role. The unprecedented flooding of the middle of America in 2019 left historic sites along the Missouri, Mississippi, and Ohio Rivers and flood plains at risk.[12] When infrastructure is lost, will securing an historic site be equal in importance to rebuilding a bridge or retooling a water treatment plant or local water and sewer lines? There are many smaller river systems across the country, and will the focus on the Midwest detract from the smaller or intrastate waterways?

These sorts of problems exist is different manifestations, everywhere. Where tornados are prevalent, similar problems have always been faced. Forest wild fires, or urban fires, have often threatened and destroyed historic structures. Similarly, small floods have their own histories.[13] There is a need to study how historic amenities were treated in wake of past disasters. What can we learn

11 *https://www.osv.org*

12 Joe Barrett and Erin Ailworth, *Facing Floods, Towns Call for New Controls on the Great Rivers*, The Wall Street Journal, May 10, 2019, *https://www.wsj.com/articles/facing-floods-towns-call-for-new-controls-on-the-great-rivers-11557480600?mod=searchresults&page=2&pos=7.*

13 The historic Ellicott City, Maryland experienced two 1000-year rain events in two years. The Ellicott City Station is a National Historic Landmark; the town dates back to 1772, with more than 200 18th century and 19th century buildings and was listed on the National Register of Historic Places in 1978. In 2016, a flood said to be a one-in-a thousand year event, damaged many of the buildings. Less than two years later, in the same area, there was even more rain. In under three hours, the Patapsco river rose over 16.5 feet to a new record high of 24.36 feet from 4:15 to 5:30 pm; the river rising nearly 3 feet every 15 minutes, going from no record to major flood stage in a little over an hour. *See* Jeff Halverson, *The Second 1000-Year Engulfed Ellicott City. Here's How it Happened,* Washington Post (May 28, 2018), *https://www.washingtonpost.com/news/capital-weather-gang/wp/2018/05/28/the-second-1000-year-rainstorm-in-two-years-engulfed-ellicott-city-heres-how-it-happened/.*

from the last century of how post-disaster relief has treated cultural heritage locally, in diverse contexts?

On the other side of the problem, what measures and legal procedures will be needed to find places to which historic buildings could be moved to, be stored or reassembled? Can plans be designed to define a community in terms of its history and its cultural heritage, and not just in terms of numbers of humans and their needs for schools and health clinics, and the commercial expansion of food stores, financial services, and other economic "growth" opportunities for new employment. The design of accommodating migration into older cities inland can be informed by the extensive experience that historic preservation has by encouraging adaptive reuse of older buildings and aligning historic preservation with neighborhood socio-economic revitalization. These measures now need to become central to programs that states, and perhaps federal agencies, will launch to move people out of harm's way.

Just as there is now a practice of adaptive reuse to integrate existing landmarks into new commercial settings, so there can be a trade in dismantling landmarks threatened with destruction from sea level rise, and incorporating their components into new structures. This reuse of the work of past artisans also could save a developer from having to acquire new building materials, and thus entitle to secure LEED "green building" credits. Preservationists will need to collaborate with urban planners to establish the criteria for this recycling of old buildings. It was done in 18th century Wellfleet, Massachusetts, and "back to the future," the practice may tomorrow be reborn as a practical way to cope with threats of sea level rise. It is probable that the costs of salvaging and relocating endangered historic structures will become part of economic real estate development, and fewer as contributions to museums or charitable endeavors of *ex situ* preservation.

There may be new assemblages of iconic historic structures of similar age or provenance in new places, such as Sturbridge Village, with its "village" setting for salvaged New England structures.[14] Perhaps preservationists will wish to encourage such salvage museums in each region of the nation, financed by tourism and historic philanthropy or local economic development interest. Should

14 Sturbridge Village, Massachusetts, *https://www.osv.org*.

the criteria for eligibility for listing on the National Register be revised to allow for *ex situ* preservation where this is the only recourse available? Can a system of "first responders" be organized to rescue damaged landmarks after disasters? Should we recreate the Works Progress Administration program to inventory landmarks at risk and prepare them for relocation? How important is saving again our preserved historic sites? Will states or the Department of Interior make provision for the intangible heritage of Indigenous Nations, and will we consult with the Indigenous Nations to learn from their intergenerational norms? These are but a few of the unknown avenues of inquiry that an era of climate change ushers in.

11D2. EXPERIMENTATION AT THE LOCAL LEVEL

Such questions are not the stuff of science fiction. They are sober inquiries, which have not yet been entertained. The socio-political denial of the phenomenon of climate change has retarded inquiry into these challenges at the level of the federal government. Preservation law exists at the level of the local governments and states. It is time for a return to the earlier periods when states were the incubators of new ideas, and cities and local governments were the laboratories for new socio-economic undertakings. When Charleston, New Orleans, Boston and New York City "invented" the first local laws to protect history, they were pioneers. Their leadership led local preservationists to compile inventories of historic sites and structures, as a prelude to designating them as sites to be protected, and then establishing landmarks commissions and standards for protecting the designated cultural assets. The same spirit of innovation in public-private partnerships and governmental stewardship is needed now, and it must begin town by town, neighborhood by neighborhood. Local leaders know their history and can frame the priorities and reasons for prioritizing heritage at risk of destruction.

11D3. INTEGRATED DISASTER PLANNING

States with historic preservation planning programs, like New York, need to boldly recast the agenda. The sightlines of planning must be raised to estimate the new physical conditions in which preservation will take place. New York's legislature has mandated the preparation of maps showing likely sea level rise at two future elevations. These maps, issued by the New York State Department of Environmental Conservation, need to become the reference points for cooperation between state recreational and parks departments and the local municipal landmarks preservation commissions and other planning authorities. Joint planning could begin to explore the fate of structures in the areas of likely future flooding and learn by doing how to plan to relocate valued older buildings in new places.

11D4. THE PAST IS THE FUTURE

No crystal ball foretells the pathways historic preservation will pursue in coming decades. If the past is prologue to the future, we can try to see how Venice has coped with its gradual inundation. We ponder in vain how physical conditions made it impossible for the Hanging Gardens of Babylon to persist in the Fertile Crescent, or why the Anasazi left their pueblos in Chaco Canyon. What roles did prolonged drought or conflict among armed communities, or epidemics, or other less plausible triggers play in closing these once robust chapters of human civilization.

What we can know is that humans in the future will value the historic record and preserved fabric we have assembled today. Stewardship of cultural heritage has saved important bits of the landscape of civilization, in living day-to-day contexts, and not just as art in museums. That living context is physically changing, but the impulse to relate to the past for the future will persist. How this may transpire, gentle readers, is for you to decide.

Additional Reading and Resources

National Register for Historic Places, *www.nps.gov/history/nr.*

Leslie E. Barras, National Trust for Historic Preservation, *Section 106 of the National Historic Preservation Act, Back to Basics* (2010).

National Park Service, U.S. Department of the Interior, State, Tribal, Local, Plans & Grants Division, Cultural Resources, Partnerships, and Science Directorate, Federal Historic Preservation Laws The Official Compilation of U.S. Cultural Heritage Statutes 2018 Edition, *https://www.nps.gov/subjects/historicpreservation/upload/NPS_FHPL_book_online.pdf*

The Historic American Buildings Survey, Recording Historic Buildings, Compiled By Harley J. Mckee, U.S. Department Of The Interior National Park Service (1970).

Preservation Organizations

Advisory Council on Historic Preservation, *www.achp.gov*

African American Heritage Preservation Foundation, *www.aahpfdn.org*

The Alliance for Historic Landscape Preservation, *www.ahlp.org*

The Alliance for National Heritage Areas, *www.nationalheritageareas.com*

American Cultural Resource Association, *www.acra-crm.org*

American Institute of Architects, *www.aia.org*

American Planning Association, *www.planning.org*

American Society of Landscape Architects, *www.asla.org*

Association for Preservation Technology International, *www.apti.org*

Conservation Online, *www.cool.conservation-us.org*

The Cultural Landscape Foundation, *www.tclf.org*

Historic Bridge Foundation, *www.historicbridgefoundation.com*

Institute for Cultural Landscape Studies, *www.icls.harvard.edu*

National Alliance of Preservation Commissions, *www.uga.edu/napc*

National Center for Preservation Technology and Training, *www.ncptt.nps.gov*

National Council of State Historic Preservation Officers, *www.ncshpo.org*

National Film Preservation Board, *lcweb.loc.gov/film/*

National Historic Landmarks Program, *www.nps.gov/history/nhl*

National Trust's Main Street, *www.preservationnation.org/main-street*

National Park Service, *www.nps.gov/history*

National Trust for Historic Preservation, *www.preservationnation.org*

Old House Network, *www.oldhousenetwork.org*

Preservation Action, *www.preservationaction.org*

Preservation Directory, *www.PreservationDirectory.com*

Preservation Magazine, *www.preservationnation.org/magazine*

Preservation Trades Network, *www.iptw.org*

PreserveNet, *www.preservenet.cornell.edu*

Rails to Trails, *www.railstotrails.org*

Partners for Sacred Places, *www.sacredplaces.org*

Scenic America, *www.scenic.org*

The Sprawl Watch Clearinghouse, *www.sprawlwatch.org*

TradeWeb, *www.tradewebdirectory.com*

Transportation Action Network, *www.transact.org*

Trust for Public Land, *www.tpl.org*

Model Ordinance

HISTORIC PRESERVATION ORDINANCE LOCAL LAW

AN ORDINANCE relating to the establishment of landmarks or historic districts in the Village/ Town/City of ___________________.

SECTION 1: PURPOSE

It is hereby declared as a matter of public policy that the protection, enhancement and perpetuation of landmarks and historic districts are necessary to promote the economic, cultural, educational, and general welfare of the public. Inasmuch as the identity of a people is founded on its past and inasmuch as ___________________ has many significant historic, architectural and cultural resources, which constitute its heritage, this act is intended to:

(A) protect and enhance the landmarks and historic districts, which represent distinctive elements of ___________________ 's historic, architectural, and cultural heritage;

(B) foster civic pride in the accomplishments of the past;

(C) protect and enhance ___________________'s attractiveness to visitors and the support and stimulus to the economy thereby provided, and insure the harmonious, orderly, and efficient growth and development of the Village/Town/City.

SECTION 2: HISTORIC PRESERVATION COMMISSION

There is hereby created a commission to be known as the ______________ ______________________ Historic Preservation Commission.

(A) The Commission shall consist of ________________________ members to be appointed, to the extent available in the community, by the mayor as follows:

> at least one shall be an architect experienced in working with historic buildings; at least one shall be a historian;
> at least one shall be a resident of a historic district;
> at least one shall have demonstrated significant interest in and commitment to the field of historic preservation evidenced either by involvement in a local historic preservation group, employment or volunteer activity in the field of historic preservation, or other serious interest in the field; and

all members shall have a known interest in historic preservation and architectural development within the Village/ Town/ City of _________.

(B) Commission members shall serve for a term of four years, with the exception of the initial term of one of the ____________________ members, which shall be one year, one, which shall be two years, and one, which shall be three years.

(C) The Chairman and Vice Chairman of the Commission shall be elected by and from among the members of the Commission.

(D) The powers of the Commission shall include:

- (i) Employment of staff and professional consultants as necessary to carry out the duties of the Commission;
- (ii) Promulgation of rules and regulations as necessary to carry out the duties of the Commission;
- (iii) Adoption of criteria for the identification of significant historic, architectural, and cultural landmarks and for the delineation of historic districts;

(iv) Conduct of surveys of significant historic, architectural, and cultural landmarks and historic districts within the Village/Town/City;

(v) Designation of identified structures or resources as landmarks and historic districts;

(vi) Acceptance on behalf of the Village/Town/City government of the donation of facade easements and development rights and the making of recommendations to the Village/Town/City government concerning the acquisition of facade easements or other interests in real property as necessary to carry out the purposes of this act;

(vii) Increasing public awareness of the value of historic, cultural and architectural preservation by developing and participating in public education programs;

(viii) Making recommendations to Village/Town/City government concerning the utilization of state, federal or private funds to promote the preservation of landmarks and historic districts within the Village/Town/City;

(ix) Recommending acquisition of a landmark structure by the Village/Town/City government where its preservation is essential to the purposes of this act and where private preservation is not feasible; and

(x) Approval or disapproval of applications for certificates of appropriateness pursuant to this act.

(E) The Commission shall meet at least monthly, but meetings may be held at any time on the written request of any two of the Commission members or on the call of the Chairman or the Mayor.

(F) A quorum for the transaction of business shall consist of ________________ of the Commission's members, but not less than a majority of the full-authorized membership may grant or deny a Certificate of Appropriateness.

SECTION 3: DESIGNATION OF LANDMARKS OR HISTORIC DISTRICTS

(A) The Commission may designate an individual property as a landmark if it:

- (i) Possesses special character or historic or aesthetic interest or value as part of the cultural, political, economic or social history of the locality, region, state or nation; or
- (ii) Is identified with historic personages; or
- (iii) Embodies the distinguishing characteristics of an architectural style; or
- (iv) Is the work of a designer whose work has significantly influenced an age; or
- (v) Because of unique location or singular physical characteristic, represents an established and familiar visual feature of the neighborhood.

(B) The Commission may designate a group of properties as a historic district if it:

- (i) contains properties which meet one or more of the criteria for designation of a landmark; and
- (ii) by reason of possessing such qualities, it constitutes a distinct section of the Village/ Town/City.

The boundaries of each historic district designated henceforth shall be specified in detail and shall be filed, in writing, in the Village/Town/City Clerk's Office for public inspection.

(C) Notice of a proposed designation shall be sent by registered mail to the owner of the property proposed for designation, describing the property and announcing a public hearing by the Commission to consider the designation. Where the proposed designation involves so many owners that individual notice is infeasible, notice may instead be published at least once in a newspaper of general circulation at least days prior to the date of the public hearing. Once the Commission has issued notice of a proposed designation, no building permits shall be issued by the building inspector until the Commission has made its decision.

(D) The Commission shall hold a public hearing prior to designation of any landmark or historic district. The Commission, owners and any interested parties may present testimony or documentary evidence at the hearing which will become part of a record regarding the historic, architectural, or cultural importance of the proposed landmark or historic district. The record may also contain staff reports, public comments, or other evidence offered outside of the hearing.

(E) The Commission shall forward notice of each property designated as a landmark and the boundaries of each designated historic district to the office of the ______________ County Clerk for recordation.

SECTION 4: CERTIFICATE OF APPROPRIATENESS FOR ALTERATION, DEMOLITION OR NEW CONSTRUCTION AFFECTING LANDMARKS OR HISTORIC DISTRICTS

No person shall carry out any exterior alteration, restoration, reconstruction, demolition, new construction, or moving of a landmark or property within a historic district, nor shall any person make any material change in the appearance of such property, its light fixtures, signs, sidewalks, fences, steps, paving or other exterior elements which affect the appearance and cohesiveness of the landmark or historic district, without first obtaining a certificate of appropriateness from the Historic Preservation Commission.

SECTION 5: CRITERIA FOR APPROVAL OF A CERTIFICATE OF APPROPRIATENESS

(A) In passing upon an application for a certificate of appropriateness, the Historic Preservation Commission shall not consider changes to interior spaces, unless they are open to the public. The Commission's decision shall be based on the following principles:

(i) properties which contribute to the character of the historic district shall be retained, with their historic features altered as little as possible;

(ii) any alteration of existing properties shall be compatible with their historic character, as well as with the surrounding district; and

(iii) new construction shall be compatible with the district in which it is located.

(B) In applying the principle of compatibility, the Commission shall consider the following factors:

(i) the general design, character and appropriateness to the property of the proposed alteration or new construction;

(ii) the scale of proposed alteration or new construction in relation to the property itself, surrounding properties, and the neighborhood;

(iii) texture, materials, and color and their relation to similar features of other properties in the neighborhood;

(iv) visual compatibility with surrounding properties, including proportion of the property's front facade, proportion and arrangement of windows and other openings within the facade, roof shape, and the rhythm of spacing of properties on streets, including setback; and

(v) the importance of historic, architectural or other features to the significance of the property.

SECTION 6: CERTIFICATE OF APPROPRIATENESS APPLICATION PROCEDURE

(A) Prior to the commencement of any work requiring a certificate of appropriateness, the owner shall file an application for such a certificate with the Historic Preservation Commission. The application shall contain:

(i) name, address and telephone number of applicant;

(ii) location and photographs of property;

(iii) elevation drawings of proposed changes, if available;

(iv) perspective drawings, including relationship to adjacent properties, if available;

(v) samples of color or materials to be used;

(vi) where the proposal includes signs or lettering, a scale drawing showing the type of lettering to be used, all dimensions and colors, a description of materials to be used, method of illumination, and a plan showing the sign's location on the property; and

(vii) any other information which the Commission may deem necessary in order to visualize the proposed work

(B) No building permit shall be issued for such proposed work until a certificate of appropriateness has first been issued by the Historic Preservation Commission. The certificate of appropriateness required by this act shall be in addition to and not in lieu of any building permit that may be required by any other ordinance of the Village/Town/City of ____________________________

(C) The Commission shall approve, deny or approve the permit with modifications within ___________________ days from receipt of the completed application. The Commission may hold a public hearing on the application at which an opportunity will be provided for proponents and opponents of the application to present their views.

(D) All decisions of the Commission shall be in writing. A copy shall be sent to the applicant by registered mail and a copy filed with the Village/Town/City Clerk's Office for public inspection. The Commission's decision shall state the reasons for denying or modifying any application.

(E) Certificates of appropriateness shall be valid for ____________ months, after which the owner must reapply if he still wishes to undertake work on the property.

SECTION 7: HARDSHIP CRITERIA FOR DEMOLITION

An applicant whose certificate of appropriateness for a proposed demolition has been denied may apply for relief on the ground of hardship. In order to prove the existence of hardship, the applicant shall establish that:

(i) the property is incapable of earning a reasonable return, regardless of whether that return represents the most profitable return possible;

(ii) the property cannot be adapted for any other use, whether by the current owner or by a purchaser, which would result in a reasonable return; and

(iii) efforts to find a purchaser interested in acquiring the property and preserving it have failed.

SECTION 8: HARDSHIP CRITERIA FOR ALTERATION

An applicant whose certificate of appropriateness for a proposed alteration has been denied may apply for relief on the ground of hardship. In order to prove the existence of hardship, the applicant shall establish that the property is incapable of earning a reasonable return, regardless of whether that return represents the most profitable return possible.

SECTION 9: HARDSHIP APPLICATION PROCEDURE

(A) After receiving written notification from the Commission of the denial of a certificate of appropriateness, an applicant may commence the hardship process. No building permit or demolition permit shall be issued unless the Commission makes a finding that a hardship exists.

(B) The Commission may hold a public hearing on the hardship application at which an opportunity will be provided for proponents and opponents of the application to present their views.

(C) The applicant shall consult in good faith with the Commission, local preservation groups and interested parties in a diligent effort to seek an alternative that will result in preservation of the property.

(D) All decisions of the Commission shall be in writing. A copy shall be sent to the applicant by registered mail and a copy filed with the Village/Town/City Clerk's Office for public inspection. The Commission's decision shall state the reasons for granting or denying the hardship application. If the application is granted, the Commission shall approve only such work as is necessary to alleviate the hardship.

SECTION 10: ENFORCEMENT

All work performed pursuant to a certificate of appropriateness issued under this ordinance shall conform to any requirements included therein. It shall be the duty of the Building Code Enforcement Officer to inspect periodically any such work to assure compliance. In the event work is found that is not being performed in accordance with the certificate of appropriateness, or upon notification of such fact by the Historic Preservation Commission, the Building Code Enforcement Officer shall issue a stop work order and all work shall immediately cease. No further work shall be undertaken on the project as long as a stop work order is in effect.

SECTION 11: MAINTENANCE AND REPAIR REQUIRED

Nothing in this ordinance shall be construed to prevent the ordinary maintenance and repair of any exterior architectural feature of a landmark or property within a historic district, which does not involve a change in design, material, color or outward appearance.

No owner or person with an interest in real property designated as a landmark or included within a historic district shall permit the property to fall into a serious state of disrepair so as to result in the deterioration of any exterior architectural feature which would, in the judgment of the Historic Preservation Commission, produce a detrimental effect upon the character of the historic district as a whole or the life and character of the property itself.

Examples of such deterioration include:

(A) Deterioration of exterior walls or other vertical supports.

(B) Deterioration of roofs or other horizontal members.

(C) Deterioration of exterior chimneys.

(D) Deterioration or crumbling of exterior stucco or mortar.

(E) Ineffective waterproofing of exterior walls, roofs or foundations, including broken windows or doors.

(F) Deterioration of any feature so as to create a hazardous condition, which could lead to the claim that demolition, is necessary for the public safety.

SECTION 12: VIOLATIONS

(A) Failure to comply with any of the provisions of this ordinance shall be deemed a violation and the violator shall be liable to a fine of not less than ________________ nor more than __________________ for each day the violation continues.

(B) Any person who demolishes, alters, constructs, or permits a designated property to fall into a serious state of disrepair in violation of this ordinance shall be required to restore the property and its site to its appearance prior to the violation. Any action to enforce this subsection shall be brought by the Village/Town/City Attorney. This civil remedy shall be in addition to and not in lieu of any criminal prosecution and penalty.

SECTION 13: APPEALS

Any person aggrieved by a decision of the Historic Preservation Commission relating to hardship or a certificate of appropriateness may, within 15 days of the decision, file a written application with the Village Board/Town Board/City Council for review of the decision. Reviews shall be conducted based on the same record that was before the Commission and using the same criteria.

Historic Preservation Commission Membership Application

Municipality/CLG:

Name:

Address:

Phone and e-mail:

Interest, competence or knowledge of historic preservation is demonstrated by: Education*:

Employment/Profession*:

Community Service*:

Memberships (e.g., historical societies):

Seminars/Workshops:

Hobbies/Interests:

Index

A

B

C

D

E

F

G

H

I

J

K

L

M

N

O

P

R

Z

About the Authors

Nicholas A. Robinson is the Distinguished University Professor and the Kerlin Environmental Law Professor, Emeritus, Pace University, where he taught Conservation Law, Advanced topics in Environmental Research, and numerous other environmental law courses. He has served as legal advisor and chairman of the Commission on Environmental Law of the International Union for the Conservation of Nature and Natural Resources, engaged in drafting treaties and counseling different countries on the preparation of their environmental laws. He is author of several books and numerous articles. He is a emeritus member of the Board of Trustees of the Jay Heritage Center. He lives and hikes in the historic village of Sleepy Hollow, New York.

Shelby D. Green is a Professor of Law at Elisabeth Haub School of Law, Pace University, White Plains, N.Y., where she teaches and writes on the subjects of Historic Preservation, Property and Real Estate Transactions & Finance. She serves on the Board of Trustees of the Jay Heritage Center, Rye, New York, and the board of directors of the Sherman Chamber Ensemble, Sherman, Connecticut.

CPSIA information can be obtained
at www.ICGtesting.com
Printed in the USA
JSHW022220170421
13665JS00001B/2

9 781600 425110